Mosaic

Compiled by

The Friends of Noel Brooks

With Dr. Chris Green, Rev. Kenneth L. Young, Irene Belyeu,

Dr. Marvin J. Hudson, and Marilyn A. Hudson

Mosaic / Norman, Oklahoma: Whorl Books.

Description: Papers in honor of the legacy of the Rev. Noel Brooks.

Subjects:

1. Religion – Addresses, essays, lectures, etc. 2. Pentecostalism-Theology — Addresses, essays, lectures, etc. 3. Brooks, Noel (1914-2006) – Criticism, interpretation, etc. 4. Mission work – Criticism, interpretation, etc. 5. Evangelism, urban – Criticism, interpretation, etc. 6. Gifts, Spiritual – Criticism, interpretation, etc. 7. Reading and books – Religious aspects- Pentecostalism – Criticism, interpretation, etc.

DEDICATION

This collection of scholarly writings – this *Gedenkschrift* - is in honor of the British born pastor, church leader, educator, and author, Noel Brooks, 1914-2006.

He was a witness to the history of Pentecostalism on two continents. He was a member of George Jeffreys Elim Pentecostal Group (writing the first biography of that man's work in Ireland and Great Britain), the Bible Pattern Fellowship and the British Pentecostal Holiness Church. Additionally, he worked with several Holiness groups.

He served as president of two Bible colleges, one in England and one in Canada. He wrote for numerous religious publications on two continents and spoke around the globe.

He left a legacy that can inform the future of both Holiness and Pentecostalism through a commitment to the compatibility of excellent scholarship and vital faith. His notable written works include, <u>Scriptural Holiness</u>, <u>Let There Be Life</u>, Let <u>There Be Life, The Biblical Basis of Missions, Ephesians,</u> and the biographical narrative, Out<u> of a Horrible Pit</u>.

CONTENTS

ACKNOWLEDGMENTS

A thank you goes to those whose support for this project was so total, strong, and unwavering. These include so many it would be impossible to name them all.

To all those who supported the idea of this project from its infancy and staunchly believe that true faith includes the totality of the human experience – mind, soul, and body – a blessing for your vision and sacrifice.

Foreword

A mosaic is an image comprised of many different pieces. Alone, the small pieces may seem insignificant and meaningless. It is as one-steps back, to view the whole that the greater truth of the image emerges.

The Friends of Noel Brooks do not claim for themselves the label of being great minds, creators of great art, or superiority in any field. What we do claim is a firm commitment to the power inherent in combining vital Christian faith with academic endeavor.

Noel Brooks rejected the false dichotomy that said one could use the mind but only at the cost of the spirit. Instead, he believed firmly mind and spirit utilized all the gifts God had given to the human creation.

Like his role model John Wesley, Brooks committed in his heart to be the best he could be for God: the best educated, the most committed, and the most serving. He did this with extreme humility because he believed God deserved no less than the best of what our minds could become.

The papers are in the spirit of celebrating a man who saw the united mind and spirit as enabling great things in the world and the church. We hope they will encourage discussion, spark thought, and initiate a hunger to have a faith in which both heart and head merge with spiritual power and purpose.

The Friends of Noel Brooks
2012

In Word and Spirit:

Critical and Constructive Reflections on

Theological Method in the Work of Noel Brooks

Chris E. Green

Noel Brooks Memorial Conference

Southwestern Christian University

March 30 2012

Introduction

The burden of this paper is to engage critically and constructively the theological method of British Pentecostal Holiness pastor and biblical theologian Noel Brooks, attempting to identify, describe, and analyze how it is that Brooks develops and articulates his (or, perhaps more accurately, his denomination's) theology.

In terms of the paper's structure, the opening section addresses what I regard as Brooks' driving concerns and aims, i.e. what it is that motivates his theological program and what he hopes to get done theologically. The second, comparatively brief section lays out his sources, identifying his main dialogue partners and explaining his use of their work. The third section is devoted to Brooks' view and use of Scripture. All that done, in the fourth and final section I venture a few critical, evaluative comments, and conclude by suggesting ways in which Noel Brooks' methodology might best be received and appropriated by Pentecostals here and now, in the church and in the academy.

Aims & Concerns:

What Did Brooks Hope to Accomplish Theologically?

Throughout his work, Brooks is concerned to give voice to Pentecostal doctrine in ways that remain true both to the witness of Scripture and to the dogmatic positions of his denomination, the International Pentecostal Holiness Church (IPHC). In spite of the fact that he frequently makes use of academic sources, he always writes accessibly, as if for a lay audience. And while his loyalty to IPHC doctrine is in every case clear, he is careful to articulate his views in ways that can be heard by Pentecostals of other traditions and non-Pentecostals as well.

To his credit, Brooks was willing to confront difficult and controversial issues.[1] In his work on healing and sickness, for instance, he acknowledges the need to "face up" to the "agonizing and gigantic" problem of those who do not receive healing.[2] Without doubt, his long experience as a pastor shaped his theological perspectives and commitments in decisive ways, so that he remained always concerned to develop theology that was not only biblically

---

[1] For example, see his defense of the classic Wesleyan-Pentecostal view of "entire sanctification" as prerequisite for receiving fullness of the Spirit in *PHA* 44.19 (Sept 3, 1960), p. 6.

[2] Noel Brooks, *Let There Be Life* (Franklin Springs, GA: Advocate Press, 1975), p. 111.

and doctrinally sound but also "realistic and practical."[3] This concern evidences itself clearly in the titles of two of Brooks' books: *Scriptural Holiness* and *Fingertip Holiness*. In the former, he is concerned to demonstrate that the IPHC position on sanctification does in fact accord with the biblical witness. In the latter, he determines to show what difference this doctrine does and does not make for the "normal" Christian life in its "everyday" expression.

As has been noted already, Brooks was a *denominational* theologian. It is usually more or less impossible to discern how, if at all, his opinion might diverge from the official doctrinal positions of the IPHC, and what, if anything, he would like to change in the articulation of those positions. That said, perhaps it would not be too much to suggest that Brooks is most uncomfortable with the IPHC doctrines at those points at which they depart from the traditional Wesleyan and Anglican positions (as he understands them).[4] For example, he has something of a problem with the statement on sin (Article 2) because it "shies off" from the language of "original guilt," which had appeared in the Anglican article and Wesley's adaptation of

---

[3] Brooks, *Let There Be Life*, p. 61.
[4] Brooks is well aware of the genealogy of the IPHC Articles of Faith, which derived from the 39 Articles of the Church of England by way of the reformulation of John Wesley. See *PHA* 53.20 (Jan 31, 1970), pp. 14-15.

it. Clearly, Brooks believes that the IPHC would do well to recover the Reformers' understanding of this term,[5] although he does not take time to explain his reasoning. This preference for the traditional (i.e. Anglican-Wesleyan) language comes clear in his brief treatment of the "ordinances" as well. Brooks rightly notes the striking difference between the denomination's statement on the Lord's Supper and the one on water baptism. In those statements "the former is described as a sacrament whereas the latter is not so described" and he observes (again, rightly) that at points the statement on the Lord's Supper seems strictly memorialist (Zwinglian). While at other points— such as in the claim that communicants "may be partakers of His nature" through their faithful celebration of the Supper—the statement comes near to the robustly sacramental "Anglican-Wesleyan" position.[6] Although muted, one detects some sense of dissatisfaction with the ambiguity of the statement on the Eucharist[7] and perhaps also with the baptistic, memorialist, "anti-sacramental" view of the washing rite put forward in the article.[8]

---

[5] *PHA* 54.5 (July 4, 1970), p. 22.
[6] *PHA* 54.24 (Mar 27, 1971), p. 14.
[7] He concludes that it is virtually impossible to "state authoritatively" the intent of the IPHC's view of the Sacrament.
[8] *PHA* 54.23 (Mar 13, 1971), p. 26.

Brooks' dissatisfaction with the language of the IPHC faith statements makes itself most evident in his critique of the IPHC statement on healing "as in the atonement." He finds the statement unclear, even misleading. "In some ways, therefore, our doctrinal statement leaves much to be desired. We might have been spared much confusion and conflict if we had been given clear guidance about these matters in our Articles of Faith."[9] One gains significant insight into Brooks' basic theological commitments, as well as into the workings of his theological method, when he insists that the lack of definition in the statement on divine healing is advantageous:

> It is interesting and important for us to observe, however, that our Article of Faith does not define what the phrase "as in the atonement" means, nor tell us in what way divine healing is in the atonement. In our opinion, this is a providential thing, for it has meant that we are not committed to the extreme and fanatical theories and practices which have grown up among some Pentecostal people through the years, and that we are free to study the Scriptures by the aid of the Holy Spirit in order to reach a clearer understanding as to what is meant by "Divine healing as in the Atonement…"[10]

---

[9] Brooks, *Let There Be Life*, p. 8.
[10] *PHA* 54.15 (Nov 21, 1970), p. 14.

Sources & Influences:

Whose Work Did Brooks Depend On—and Why?

Besides Scripture, Brooks makes frequent and extensive use of a wide range of theological sources, both popular and academic.[11] For obvious reasons, he appeals often to IPHC figures, including most often W.H. Turner,[12] J.E. Campbell,[13] J.N. Holmes,[14] J.H. King[15] and J.A. Synan.[16] Brooks draws on the work of Pentecostals from other denominations and movements as well, including Donald Gee's reflections on the *charismata*[17] and George Jeffreys' book, *Pentecostal Rays*.[18]

---

[11] Besides biblical and theological sources, Brooks also often engages the soft and hard sciences as well, including, for instance, psychiatry, psychology, history, and philosophy.

[12] *PHA* 54.9 (Aug 29, 1970), pp. 14-15; *PHA* 54.11 (Sep 26, 1970), pp. 18-19; *PHA* 54.13 (Oct 24, 1970), pp. 14-15; *PHA* 54.13 (Oct 24, 1970), pp. 14-15; Brooks, *Sickness, Health, and God*, p. 11.

[13] *PHA* 54.9 (Aug 29, 1970), pp. 14-15.

[14] *PHA* 54.19 (Jan 16, 1971), p. 14; *PHA* 54.9 (Aug 29, 1970), pp. 14-15; Brooks, *Scriptural Holiness,* p. 58.

[15] Brooks, *Let There Be Life*, p. 13; Brooks, *Sickness, Health, and God*, pp. 51-52; *PHA* 54.9 (Aug 29, 1970), pp. 14-15; *PHA* 54.11 (Sep 26, 1970), pp. 18-19; *PHA* 54.16 (Dec 5, 1970), pp. 14-15; *PHA* 54.16 (Dec 5, 1970), pp. 14-15;

[16] *PHA* 54.8 (Aug 15, 1970), pp. 14-15; *PHA* 54.13 (Oct 24, 1970), pp. 14-15; *PHA* 54.16 (Dec 5, 1970), pp. 14-15; *PHA* 54.17 (Dec 19, 1970), pp. 14-15; *PHA* 54.20 (Jan 30, 1971), pp. 14-15;

[17] *PHA* 54.13 (Oct 24, 1970), pp. 14-15; *PHA* 54.22 (Feb 27, 1971), p. 14; Brooks, *Sickness, Health, and God*, p. 15.

[18] Noel Brooks, *Sickness, Health, and God* (Franklin Springs, GA: Advocate Press, 1965), p. 10; Brooks, *Let There Be Life*, pp. 37, 58, 75; *PHA* 54.11 (Sep 26, 1970), p. 19; *PHA* 54.13 (Oct 24, 1970), pp. 14-15.

Brooks had a firm grasp of the writings of the Wesley brothers, and he appealed to them often—particularly John's sermons.[19] What is more, he was conversant with a number of theologians in the Wesleyan-Methodist tradition, including Samuel Chadwick,[20] J.S. Banks,[21] G.S. Turner,[22] Daniel Steele,[23] W.E. Sangster,[24] and W.B. Pope.[25] Evangelical Anglicans serve as important dialogue partners for him as well (e.g. William Temple,[26]

---

[19] Noel Brooks, *Fingertip Holiness: Studies in Practical Holiness* (Franklin Springs, GA: Advocate Press, 1975), pp. 30, 56. See also Noel Brooks, *Scriptural Holiness* (Franklin Springs, GA: Advocate Press, 1967), pp. 24-25, 57, 61, 67; *PHA* 54.19 (Jan 16, 1971), p. 14; *PHA* 54.7 (Aug 1, 1970), pp. 14-15; *PHA* 54.8 (Aug 15, 1970), pp. 14-15; *PHA* 54.9 (Aug 29, 1970), pp. 14-15; *PHA* 54.11 (Sep 26, 1970), pp. 18-19; *PHA* 54.21 (Feb 13, 1971), p. 14.

[20] Brooks, *Scriptural Holiness*, p. 66; *PHA* 54.10 (Sep 12, 1970), pp. 14-15; *PHA* 54.11 (Sep 26, 1970), pp. 18-19; Brooks, *Sickness, Health, and God*, p. 19

[21] Brooks, *Scriptural Holiness*, p. 50; *PHA* 53.22 (Feb 28, 1970), pp. 22-23.

[22] *PHA* 54.9 (Aug 29, 1970), pp. 14-15.

[23] Brooks, *Scriptural Holiness*, pp. 38, 45; *PHA* 54.12 (Oct 10, 1970), pp. 18-19.

[24] Noel Brooks, *Sickness, Health, and God* (Franklin Springs, GA: Advocate Press, 1965), p. 10; Brooks, *Scriptural Holiness*, pp. 60-61, 64; *Fingertip Holiness*, pp. 33, 39, 48; *PHA* 54.10 (Sep 12, 1970), pp. 14-15; *PHA* 54.11 (Sep 26, 1970), pp. 18-19.

[25] *PHA* 54.1 (May 9, 1970), p. 15; *PHA* 54.7 (Aug 1, 1970), pp. 14-15; *PHA* 54.18 (Jan 30, 1971), p. 15; *PHA* 54.22 (Feb 27, 1971), p. 14; Brooks, *Scriptural Holiness*, pp. 45, 48.

[26] Brooks, *Fingertip Holiness*, p. 25; Brooks, *Let There Be Life*, pp. 29-30.

Handley Moule,[27] his nephew, C.D.F. Moule,[28] and, perhaps more than the others, W.H. Griffith Thomas).[29]

He commanded knowledge of many sources from the Reformed tradition(s) as well, including Bible commentators (e.g. Matthew Henry,[30] William Barclay,[31] F.F. Bruce,[32] and Leon Morris[33]), devotional writers (e.g. A.W. Tozer[34] and Andrew Murray[35]), and preachers (e.g. G.C. Campbell[36] and D. Martin Lloyd Jones).[37] In his own doctrinal writings, Brooks routinely appeals to the work of Reformed theologians, too, including John Calvin,[38] John Owen,[39] Jonathan Edwards,[40] Abraham Kuyper,[41] William

---

[27] *PHA* 54.19 (Jan 16, 1971), p. 14; *PHA* 54.21 (Feb 13, 1971), p. 14.

[28] Brooks, *Scriptural Holiness,* p. 56; *PHA* 54.1 (May 9, 1970), pp. 14-15; *PHA* 54.9 (Aug 29, 1970), pp. 14-15.

[29] *PHA* 53.21 (Feb 14, 1970), pp. 22-23; *PHA* 54.8 (Aug 15, 1970), pp. 14-15; *PHA* 54.16 (Dec 5, 1970), pp. 14-15; *PHA* 54.18 (Jan 30, 1971), p. 15.

[30] *PHA* 44.19 (Sept 3, 1960), p. 6; *Fingertip Holiness*, pp. 36, 44, 46; Brooks, *Sickness, Health, and God*, p. 10.

[31] Brooks, *Fingertip Holiness*, pp. 18, 25, 35, 59, 66; PHA 54.15 (Nov 21, 1970), p. 14.

[32] Brooks, *Fingertip Holiness*, pp. 7-8, 14.

[33] *PHA* 53.22 (Feb 28, 1970), p. 23; *PHA* 53.25 (Apr 11, 1970), p. 18.

[34] Brooks, *Scriptural Holiness,* p. 59.

[35] Brooks, *Scriptural Holiness,* p. 45; PHA 54.15 (Nov 21, 1970), p. 14.

[36] Brooks, *Fingertip Holiness*, p. 46; Brooks, *Let There Be Life*, p. 107

[37] Brooks, *Let There Be Life*, pp. 17-19, 48

[38] Brooks, *Sickness, Health, and God*, p. 66.

[39] *PHA* 54.8 (Aug 15, 1970), pp. 14-15.

[40] Brooks, *Scriptural Holiness,* p. 45.

Evans,[42] Lewis Sperry Chafer,[43] James Orr,[44] C.H. Dodd,[45] and J.I. Packer.[46] The systematic theologies of A.H. Strong,[47] Charles Hodge,[48] and Louis Berkhof[49] seem to hold a pride of place in Brooks' thinking, as does B.B. Warfield's account of the inspiration and infallibility of sacred Scripture.[50]

---

[41] Brooks, *Scriptural Holiness*, pp. 41-42.

[42] *PHA* 53.18 (Jan 3, 1970), pp. 13-14; *PHA* 53.20 (Jan 31, 1970), pp. 14-15.

[43] *PHA* 54.23 (Mar 13, 1971), p. 26; *PHA* 54.5 (July 4, 1970), p. 22; *PHA* 54.16 (Dec 5, 1970), pp. 14-15;

[44] Brooks, *Sickness, Health, and God*, p. 37; Brooks, *Let There Be Life*, p. 14; *PHA* 53.20 (Jan 31, 1970), pp. 14-15; *PHA* 54.8 (Aug 15, 1970), pp. 14-15.

[45] Brooks, *Scriptural Holiness*, p. 8; Brooks, *Fingertip Holiness*, p. 14.

[46] Brooks, *Sickness, Health, and God*, pp. 78-79.

[47] Brooks, *Sickness, Health, and God*, p. 73; Brooks, *Scriptural Holiness*, p. 45; *PHA* 53.18 (Jan 3, 1970), pp. 13-14; PHA 54.2 (May 23, 1970), p. 15; *PHA* 53.21 (Feb 14, 1970), pp. 22-23; *PHA* 54.6 (July 18, 1970), p. 14; *PHA* 54.7 (Aug 1, 1970), pp. 14-15; *PHA* 54.16 (Dec 5, 1970), pp. 14-15; *PHA* 54.21 (Feb 13, 1971), p. 14; *PHA* 54.22 (Feb 27, 1971), p. 14; *PHA* 54.22 (Feb 27, 1971), p. 14.

[48] Brooks, *Fingertip Holiness*, p. 39, 41, 49-50; *PHA* 54.2 (May 23, 1970), p. 15; *PHA* 53.21 (Feb 14, 1970), pp. 22-23.

[49] *PHA* 53.18 (Jan 3, 1970), pp. 13-14; *PHA* 53.20 (Jan 31, 1970), pp. 14-15; *PHA* 54.2 (May 23, 1970), p. 15; *PHA* 54.3 (June 6, 1970), p. 15; *PHA* 54.19 (Jan 16, 1971), p. 14; *PHA* 53.21 (Feb 14, 1970), pp. 22-23; *PHA* 54.6 (July 18, 1970), p. 14; *PHA* 54.7 (Aug 1, 1970), pp. 14-15; *PHA* 54.20 (Jan 30, 1971), p. 15; Brooks, *Scriptural Holiness*, p. 41.

[50] In his *Scriptural Holiness* (p. 8), Brooks describes Warfield as an "outstanding authority," and even when he strongly disagrees with Warfield about the possibility of divine healing (see *PHA* 54.13 [Oct 24, 1970], pp. 14-15; *PHA* 54.15 [Nov 21, 1970], p. 14; Brooks, *Let There Be Life*, pp. 24-27) and the "amillenial" view of Christ's "second coming" (see *PHA* 54.16 [Dec 5, 1970], pp. 14-15), he nonetheless engages him deferentially, with obvious respect. He is most dependent

Not unaware of the diversity of his resources,
Brooks makes it clear that he desires to bring these various
voices into harmony both with one another and with
"scriptural revelation."[51] In his estimation, such a
harmonization is both desirable and possible because the
Wesleyan tradition itself is a "synthesis of the Calvinistic and
Arminian schemes, or, in other words, a synthesis of
universal depravity (which is the Calvinistic view of human
nature) and universal grace (which is the Arminian view of
the atonement)."[52] In fact, this move toward convergence
may be one of the key features of his theological *modus
operandi.*

A final word about Brooks' theological sources: he
depended almost entirely on Protestant sources. At times, he
evinces a dislike for "Romanism."[53] He *does* appeal to
Fenelon, a French Catholic mystic,[54] and he appreciates that

---

on Warfield in his doctrine of Scripture; see *PHA* 54.1 (May 9, 1970),
pp. 14-15.

[51] Brooks, *Scriptural Holiness*, pp. 45-46.

[52] Brooks, *Scriptural Holiness*, pp. 42-43. Brooks rejects
"particular election, limited atonement, and the "special efficacious call
to the elect," as well as the notion that regeneration is the first event of
the *ordo salutis.*

[53] See, for example, *PHA* 54.24 (Mar 27, 1971), p. 14.

[54] Brooks, *Fingertip Holiness*, p. 68.

RCC's examination of alleged healings and hopes the IPHC adopts a similar system.[55]

Truth & Hermeneutics:

How Did Brooks View and Use Scripture?

As has been seen, Brooks was widely read in various doctrinal traditions. However, in the final analysis, Brooks is perhaps best described as a *biblical* theologian.[56] He considered his ultimate responsibility as a theologian to be to witness of the sacred text. For him, Scripture serves as the "ultimate seat of authority in religion." In his own words, "It is not the Bible as judged by the human reason which is authoritative, or the Bible as interpreted by the Church, but the Bible itself."[57] In this connection, he cites the opinion of Bishop Handley Moule:

> It is important to observe that authority may be real, yet not ultimate. A Creed has authority; a council has authority; a Father has authority, and still more, many consenting Fathers, witnessing to facts of belief. But none of these has ultimate authority. The Scriptures have it.[58]

---

[55] Brooks, *Let There Be Life*, p. 54.
[56] Certainly, this is the best fit of the types outlined by Christopher A. Stephenson in his *Types of Pentecostal Theology: Method, System, and Spirit* (New York: Oxford University Press, 2012).
[57] *PHA* 54.2 (May 23, 1970), p. 15.
[58] *PHA* 54.2 (May 23, 1970), p. 15.

In spite of the fact that Brooks appeals to Moule's method as exemplary, he does not actually adhere to it himself. For whatever reason, the councils, creeds, and Patristic sources have at best a marginal place in Brooks' theology—even as penultimate authorities. He does trace the history of the doctrine of the "personality" of the Holy Spirit through the Nicene Creed, where he follows the standard Evangelical view in affirming the *filioque*,[59] and he also appeals to the creeds in his description of the doctrine of the church, drawing on the classic *ecclesiae notae*.[60] But he does not make substantial use of the creeds as authoritative. In his handling of the doctrine of God, Brooks affirms that the Bible alone affords all that needs to be believed: "How do we know God is like this? From where do we derive this information? From the Bible. The Bible embodies the supernatural Self-disclosure of God. It is our source-book of doctrine."[61]

Of course, to say that one holds a "high" view of sacred Scriptures does not say anything about one's hermeneutic; there remains always the possibility of disjunction between what one says about the Scriptures and

---

[59] *PHA* 53.25 (Apr 11, 1970), p. 18.
[60] *PHA* 54.20 (Jan 30, 1971), p. 15. He insists that it is "obvious" that "no institution on earth can lay claim to these 'notes.'" They apply exclusively to the "invisible" church.
[61] *PHA* (Jan 3, 1970), p. 14

how one in fact uses them. How does Brooks use Scripture? One of the defining features of Brooks hermeneutic is his attention to what John Wesley called the "whole tenor" of Scripture.[62] In a word, Brooks' hermeneutic is *canonical*—and, needless to say, he assumes the Protestant canon as authoritative. So, for example, in his 1967 King Memorial Lectures entitled "Scriptural Holiness," Brooks devotes an entire lecture to holiness/sanctification in the Old Testament and he follows a kind of canonical logic, so that the lecture on the Old Testament begins with a section entitled "Holiness in Patriarchal Times," moves to a section on holiness in the "Mosaic Legislation," then to holiness in the prophets, and concludes with a section devoted to holiness in the wisdom and poetic literature. He does much the same in the lecture on the New Testament.

Another of the more telling features of Brooks' hermeneutic is his use of "word study." Throughout his work, he draws extensively on Vine's *Expository Dictionary* and Kittles' *TDNT* as well as the *Expositor's Greek Testament*, and utilizes a number of English translations, including *inter alia* the RSV, NEB, Weymouth, Moffatt, and Phillips.[63]

---

[62] In the words of Joel B. Green (*Reading Scripture as Wesleyans* [Nashville: Abingdon, 2010], p. 29), "John Wesley read each part of Scripture as an aspect of the whole of Scripture."

[63] See for example how he uses these resources in his exegesis of 1 Corinthians 13 (Brooks, *Fingertip Holiness*, pp. 39-52).

Informed by these resources and others like them, Brooks attempts to home in on the exact meaning of this or that biblical term in its "original language," and thereby to arrive at God's words. At times, especially in his development of the doctrine of sanctification, Brooks makes this or that word to bear heavy theological weight. For the sake of space, one example must suffice: in making the point that "holiness of heart is attained by a gradual process" that finds its "crux" in a "definite spiritual crisis of cleansing and consecration," Brooks appeals to a single biblical text, 2 Cor. 7.1. Pointing out that the word "cleanse" (καθαρίσωμεν) is in the *aorist* tense while the word "perfecting" (ἐπιτελοῦντες) is in the *present continuous*, he concludes that "thus Paul appeals for a *crisis* of cleansing and a *process* of perfecting."[64] This feature of Brooks' hermeneutic is "telling" because it points to his commitment to a Princetonian/fundamentalist understanding of biblical inspiration, authority, and efficiency, and to a grammatical-historical hermeneutic. [65]

---

[64] Brooks, *Scriptural Holiness,* p. 37; see also, Brooks, *Fingertip Holiness*, pp. 11-13.

[65] According to Bruce Corley, Steve Lemke, and Grant Lovejoy (eds.), *Biblical Hermeneutics: A Comprehensive Guide to Interpreting Scripture* (2nd ed.; Nashville: Broadman & Holman, 2002), p. 125, "Princeton's methods of scriptural interpretation relied heavily on the principles of Scottish common sense philosophy. Their defense of scriptural authority was based upon the notion the empirical induction is the primary source of truth and that all reasonable people

Like all readers of Scripture,[66] Brooks comes to the text with a hermeneutical lens, a theological "frame of reference" that makes coherent interpretation possible. According to Brooks, interpreters of Scripture must always account for the fact of "progressive revelation," a *schema* Brooks believes is revealed in Scripture (Galatians 3.23-25 and Hebrews 1.1-3).[67] So, in his lectures on "Scriptural Holiness," Brooks writes:

> I believe that the Bible is the inspired record of God's revelation to man. There is progress in that revelation, but it is progress from truth to a greater

---

intuit moral absolutes. They defined theology as a science, mining the Scriptures for facts much like a scientist gathers data from nature." Similarly, Stanley Grenz (*Renewing the Center: Evangelical Theology in a Post-Theological Era* [Grand Rapids: Baker Academic, 2006], p. 78) observes the same phenomena: "Lying behind the Princeton theology was the Scottish common sense realism devised by Thomas Reid and imported to Princeton by John Witherspoon... On American soil, this view entailed the principle that knowledge requires the assumption of the basic reliability of the human senses to perceive objects as they actually exist, together with the ability of the mind to classify the evidence so gleaned and carefully organize it into facts about the world... Convinced that theology and science shared a common empirical and inductive method, Hodge patterned his work after that of the scientist. Just as the natural scientist offers this assessment: uncovers the facts pertaining to the natural world, he asserted, so the theologian brings to light the theological facts found within the Bible. And these facts are uncovered through the application of the inductive method to the Scriptures. Hodge's appropriation of the reigning scientific model also affected how he viewed the products of his labors. He assumed that the theological propositions they drew from the Bible stated universal, even eternal, facts."

[66] Whether knowingly or not.

[67] *PHA* 54.3 (June 6, 1970), p. 14.

expression of truth. This is a principle that applies to all the great truths of Scripture...[68]

In Brooks' view, the biblical "truth of holiness"—by which he means, generally, the unbroken loyalty to and unstinting love for Christ the Wesleys had described as "entire sanctification,"[69] and, specifically, the experience of sanctification as a "second definite work of grace," which he believes is taught fully only in the NT epistles[70]—was given, like all divine truths, "in fragmentary and varied fashion in the Old Testament times, until finally God spoke His crowning about it in Christ His beloved Son."[71] If one were to read the Bible without understanding this truth, then one would unavoidably "mishandle" the word of truth, wrongly dividing it.

---

[68] Brooks, *Scriptural Holiness,* p. 9.
[69] Brooks, *Scriptural Holiness,* p. 40.
[70] Brooks, *Scriptural Holiness,* p. 37.
[71] Brooks, *Scriptural Holiness,* pp. 9-10.

Affirmation & Critique:

What Are We to Make of Brooks' Theological Method?

I find much to praise in the method that shapes and animates Brooks' theology. First, it is to his credit that he puts his skills and knowledge to work in service of the IPHC, narrowly, and the Pentecostal and Evangelical movements, more broadly. After all, one cannot do theology from nowhere, and in spite of what many people wish were true, no generic form of the faith ("mere" Christianity) exists. One must have roots in this or that spiritual/doctrinal tradition.

Second, Brooks is to be commended for his championing of Scripture's authority, and, just as importantly, for his close reading of biblical passages and his attentiveness to the canonical sweep of Scripture.

Third, he is due recognition for his engagement with a host of dialogue partners, both from within and from without Pentecostal circles, and for his attempt to harmonize, to bring into a kind of conceptual at-one-ment, various Reformed and Arminian views of soteriology.

All that praise notwithstanding, some aspects of Brooks' methodology do strike me as problematic, or at least puzzling. In what follows, I want to characterize these features—briefly and charitably—not to disparage or to disrespect his work, but only to cast light on our own theological processes.

First, I wish Brooks had read theologians of other "tribes" with greater sympathy and care. One cannot read everything, of course, but I wonder what Brooks might have learned from the insights of his contemporaries (say, Barth, Tillich, Bonhoeffer, or von Balthasar), to say nothing of ancient and medieval theologians? What if he had read not only the Wesleys but also, say, Ignatius or the Cappadocians, as John Wesley himself did?

Second, I wonder if Brooks' hermeneutic is not overly dependent on "word study"? If one were to strip away this technique from his theology of healing, his basic claims might well stand unchanged. However, if taken away from his theology of *holiness*, what would remain?

Third, I hold serious reservations with the Princetonian view of Scripture that underlies and guides his theological method and hermeneutic. As Ken Archerd[72] and others have shown, this model is fraught with intractable

---

[72] Kenneth J. Archer, *A Pentecostal Hermeneutic: Spirit, Scripture, and Community* (Cleveland, TN: CPT Press, 2009).

problems. Has Brooks placed Scripture in the place of Christ?[73]

Third, while no one can question Brooks' loyalty to the doctrines of the IPHC and to the Wesleyan-Pentecostal tradition, it nonetheless remains at least possible that his *theological method* is essentially at odds with Pentecostal spirituality. At the level of methodology, Brooks is perhaps more Evangelical than Pentecostal. Is he fighting in Saul's armor?[74]

Fourth, I previously praised Brooks for his dedication to the doctrines of the IPHC, and I want to do nothing to retract that praise. Still, it is fair to ask if he navigates well the way between being true to the denomination's theological claims on the one hand and to the claims of "the faith once delivered to the saints"[75] on the other hand. Put differently, it appears that his work is at

---

[73] Heb. 1.1-3, after all, does not say that God has spoken a final word in the Scripture, but in the *Son*. In my judgment, Brooks goes wrong in speaking of Scripture as "the supernatural Self-disclosure of God." Only Jesus, the Word, holds this place in the order of revelation, as John 1 makes clear.

[74] Even if so, I agree with Stephenson (*Types of Pentecostal Theology: Method, System, and Spirit*, pp. 240-41) that there is no reason to discredit the work of Pentecostals who depend on the language and doctrinal categories of other traditions, for Saul did in fact slay his thousands.

[75] That is, the orthodox liturgico-dogmatic tradition to which all Christians are called to devote themselves.

certain points in danger of being too sectarian, and so holds little ecumenical promise.

Some Pentecostals, perhaps, will not agree that Brooks' sectarianism is problematic. However, it seems clear to me that Pentecostals, like all Christians, are called to seek the visible unity of the church catholic, both in terms of doctrine and *praxis*. Moreover, that theology, therefore, must be done with the ecumene in mind. In my judgment, Cecil Robeck Jr. has it right:

> Theology and the work of doing theology belong to the whole Church. It cannot be done without dialogue. It must be done in relation to the whole Church in the whole world... [Therefore,] it is time for Pentecostals and Charismatic Christians of all kinds to look at the masses around them and ask what kind of theology the whole Church needs... Sectarianism is only as good as its ability to lose itself once again in the whole Church while it raises to our consciousness a long overlooked truth of the Gospel. To dwell too long in the land of sectarianism is to move toward the horizon of heresy.[76]

---

[76] Cecil M. Robeck, Jr., "Doing Theology in Isolation" *Pneuma* 12.1 (Spr 1990), p. 3.

Conclusion

What, then, are we as Pentecostal scholars and practitioners to do? How can and should we receive Brooks' theology—and the method that orders and sustains it? I suggest that above all we learn to receive them in such a way that we can put our theology into the service of the whole church as well as the Pentecostal tradition.[77] To that end, we must figure how to factor the creeds, councils, and writings of the church fathers into the heart of our theological method. Moreover, we must continue to re-envision what it means for Scripture to be authoritative as the "norming norm" of all other theological sources. Imitating Brooks, we must continue to do theology from our "roots" in the Pentecostal theological and spiritual tradition, and, most importantly, we must continue to be animated by the same spirit of patience, gentleness, and love for the truth. Only in this way can we hope to do justice to Brooks' legacy.

---

[77] More and more Pentecostals are calling for this ecumenical sensitivity and engagement. See, for example, Louis William Oliverio, "Theological Hermeneutics in the Classical Pentecostal Tradition: A Typological Account" (PhD diss.; Marquette University, 2009); Wolfgang Vondey, *Beyond Pentecostalism*: *The Crisis of Global Christianity and the Renewal of the Theological Agenda* (Grand Rapids: Eerdmans, 2010).

INVESTING IN THE CITY:

PAUL AND ROMANS A PARADIGM

Kenneth L. Young
Southwestern Christian University

A late afternoon radio advertisement interrupts the joyful sounds of Christmas music. "Make an investment in Oklahoma City; vote 'yes' on the bond issue!"[1] The familiar voice of Mayor Mick Cornett reverberates through the vehicle as he champions the cause of increasing the tax base of the city by upgrading the infrastructure and, subsequently, enticing new businesses.

His message accentuates the growth while reminding the listeners of unsafe bridges over waterways, uneven pavement on roads, and unfinished plans for downtown development. The interruption agitates this writer, but the thought of investing in the city intrigues him. Arriving at his destination provides another interruption; this author must prepare for his class on the *Letter of Paul to the Romans*.

As he rehearses the possible and probable reasons for Paul's writing to the Roman believers, he notes the prominence of the themes of investment, risk, and benefits. Paul begins and ends his letter with these themes. This information, consequently, causes this writer to ponder how Paul and *Romans* might inform us regarding when, where, why, and how people might invest in cities generally and in Oklahoma City particularly. Does this letter identify additional methods of investments? Does it present other and better ways to invest in the city? Does it denote the risk or risks one encounters through this type of investment? Does it reveal any benefits from such an investment? Does it illustrate how the Church, the body of Christ, might contribute to this investment? Could this ancient letter serve as a contemporary paradigm for investment opportunities of the magnitude needed in our cities? This writer answers affirmatively these questions. Therefore, this manuscript intends to expose how Paul, the ancient city of Rome, and *The Letter of Romans* offer contemporary society a paradigm of philosophical and theological bases as well as identify pragmatic challenges (risks) and beneficial solutions for investing in the city.

In the aforementioned advertisement, the Mayor of Oklahoma City focuses his investment plan on infrastructure – things. The thoughts of this listener began to deliberate on people. Will the wider highways infringe upon the cardboard homes of some of its citizens? Will the new or improved bridges offer the same newness or improvement to those who live under them? Will the new high-rise buildings force homeless shelters out of the area or out of business? The gospel to which Paul refers in Romans 1:16 offers answers to the need for new infrastructure and the need to care for people. Bakke, in agreement with Temple, states, "we Christians are the only people who can truly discuss the salvation of souls and the rebuilding of city sewer systems in the same sentence."[2] The gospel fulfills the objective need of the city and the subjective need of the citizen. The challenges in Rome during the ministry of Paul (circa 36-66/67 C.E.) and the reigns of Claudius (41-54 C.E.) and Nero (54-68 C.E.) are quite similar.

By the middle of the first century, Rome boasted a population approaching one million. "The population probably passed the million mark about this time, and the city was as cosmopolitan as New York and London."[3] This number includes the slave population. Despite their objectionable demeanors both Claudius and Nero recognized that such a large populace required changes in the infrastructure of the city. Claudius began at the executive level. "Claudius reorganized the civil administration of the government."[4] Thus, he prepared leadership for the managerial affairs of the city. In some ways, he surpassed even the reign of Augustus. He finally conquered Britain. He built a port at Ostia in order to bring a Mediterranean harbor closer to Rome. Some of his decisions were unpopular, but they demonstrated his administrative prowess.

Nero, too, inherited an unfavorable reputation due in part to his local persecution of Christians; yet, he favored city improvements, especially ones such as the fine arts and the Greek games. After the great fire of Rome, "Nero provided funds to help private persons rebuild and set up a kind of fire code requiring building setbacks and such to make the reconstructed city safer from fire."[5] His motive was personal gain, but his methods proved industrious. Nero also verified his ability in human resources. "He chose good men for important jobs in the provinces, the best examples being Vespasian for the Jewish rebellion and, earlier, Corbulo for a general command against the Parthians, where the struggle involved the control of Armenia...."[6] One particular decision, however, enacted by Claudius and rescinded later by Nero, affected significantly the city of Rome and the Church there.

In 49 C.E., Claudius expelled the Jews from Rome. According to Suetonius, the Emperor based his decision on their "rebellious acts with regard to one named Chrestus."[7] This edict affected five percent of the population or approximately 50,000 Jews who were living in Rome. It changed essentially the composition of the Roman community in general and the local churches in particular. Udo Schnelle analyzes the impact on the local congregation.

The edict of Claudius not only affected the Roman Jews but was also important in several respects for the Christian community there: (1) The edict effected the final separation of Christians from the synagogue. (2) The expulsion of Jews and Jewish Christians from Rome had a decisive effect on the composition of the Christian congregations there. (3) The edict had probably prevented Paul from coming to Rome earlier....(4) The edict made it clear to the young Christian community that they would have to find their own way in the field of conflicting forces between the synagogue and the Roman authorities.[8]

Yet, this imperial action made possible the encounter between Paul and the ministry team of Aquila and Priscilla! "And he found a certain Jew named Aquila, a native of Pontus, having recently come from Italy, and with him Priscilla, his wife, because Claudius had ordered all the Jews to leave Rome" (Acts 18:2).[9] After Nero ascended to the emperorship he repealed the edict of Claudius, thus granting Jews and Jewish Christians the opportunity to return to Rome. Priscilla and Aquila returned after serving in Ephesus. Concomitantly, Paul purposes to visit Rome. "After these things were finished Paul said, 'I must also see Rome.'"[10] In response to Nero's revocation of the edict and in preparation for his planned visit to the imperial city, Paul composed his letter to the churches in Rome in 57 C.E. during his stay at Corinth. Why Rome? What attracted Paul to this urban center?

Paul recognized the opportunities now available to him. Though Rome was located in Italy and capital of the Roman Empire, it was not immune to the effects of Hellenization. "Rome merely reorganized and centralized these Greek social and cultural realities, and the milieu spread throughout Palestine and in the whole Near East."[11] Alexander the Great unified the western and near eastern world; Rome stabilized and solidified it. Romans possessed a propensity for acquiring and enhancing the best of other cultures. Paul exploited this aspect of Roman civilization in order to propagate the Gospel. As sociologist Rodney Stark hypothesizes, "Paul concentrated on the more Hellenized cities" (of which Rome was one), and "Paul tended to missionize cities with substantial Jewish Diasporan communities."[12] According to his analyses, there is a one hundred to one probability of accuracy.[13] Accordingly, Paul targets Rome. His vision for Rome and his resolve to go there supports the idea of Conn and Ortiz that the city shapes theology.[14] The imperial city shaped the superlative theology in the letter, which Paul composes.

Paul capitalizes on his planned visit to Rome and the probable schism resulting from the influx of the returning Jewish Christians. Their homecoming affected the composition of the churches there as much as the original edict. If the edict "left a vacuum in the early community which the Gentile believers came to fill,"[15] then its revocation and the subsequent reentry of the Jewish Christians almost certainly challenged the philosophical and theological underpinnings of the Roman churches in addition to their practical existence. The repatronization of the Roman churches presented Paul the opportunity to discuss these vital issues relative to Jewish and Gentile believers. Paul recognized the investment, considered the risks, and anticipated the benefits of reaching Rome. He accepted enthusiastically the challenge to respond.

Paul reveals his motive for visiting Rome in segments of the thanksgiving (Romans 1:8-15) and the concluding formula (Romans 15:14-16:27) of the letter, and he uses the language of investment, risk, and benefit. "For I yearn to see you in order that I may impart some spiritual gift to you that you may be established; moreover, that I may be encouraged along with you by our mutual faith, both yours and mine. I do not want you to be unknowing, brothers (and sisters) that often I purposed to come to you, (and I have been prevented even to this time), in order that I may realize some fruit (benefit) also among you in proportion to the rest of the Gentiles."[16] He seeks mutual partnership with the churches there. Paul elucidates his aspiration to visit Rome with three purpose clauses. His intentions include investing in the believers with an undisclosed "spiritual gift," giving and receiving mutual encouragement, and obtaining some benefit. Paul conceals the exact nature of his investment and their return by his use of the indefinite pronoun "some." The verbiage may be elusive, but the idea is clear: Paul intends to invest in and reap a benefit from the Christians in Rome. This partnership will involve mutual investments, risks, and benefits. Hence, he arranges his theology around this theme.

Paul clarifies the introductory language in the conclusion of his letter. After reiterating his ardor to visit Rome temporarily while on his way to Spain (15:23), he states, "For when journeying through I hope to see you and to be sent there (Spain) by you after I have first benefited from our time together." [17] Paul repeats this same proposition in 15:28, plausibly for emphasis. He realized the tactical advantage of cities in general and of Rome in particular. "They were strategic centers, not cloisters, from which the gospel would be spread." [18] Paul employed this tactic throughout his career.

Along with Barnabas, he began in Antioch, Syria. As the gospel spread westward, he selected Corinth for his base in Greece and Macedonia. "He stayed (here) a year and six months, teaching the word of God among them."[19] On his return to Antioch Paul passed through Ephesus, leaving Priscilla and Aquila there while he journeyed to Jerusalem to greet the church there and then to Antioch to report on his mission. He returned to Ephesus where he settled "for two years, so that all who lived in Asia heard the word of the Lord, both Jews and Greeks."[20] According to Luke, this tactic produced remarkable results. From Ephesus Paul saturated Asia (Minor) with the gospel, reaching even to Colossae, a city that Paul never visited! He understood the advantage of urban centers.

It was this urban setting with its common language, its spirit of ecumenism, its willingness to experiment, its accessibility by both land and sea, its concentrations of people, its spiritual ferment, its competing myths and its interaction with other cities that formed the setting – some would say the perfect setting – for Paul's mission. Some before him and others after him concentrated their proselytizing in the cities. Apparently, though, none was as successful as Paul was in understanding the urban culture, nor as adept as he in exploiting the opportunities it provided for preaching the gospel.[21]

What better urban setting than the capital city of the empire, Rome, to reach the periphery of the known world! The time was appropriate; the opportunity was available. Paul invested in the city of Rome, in the gospel message incorporated in his letter to the Romans, and in the people there.

Paul knows that he possesses the apposite capital for an investment of this magnitude. He has the spiritual and the human resources, the gospel of Jesus Christ and the Christian community at Rome, to ensure success. Paul decides not to neglect this supreme opportunity. His motive issues from a deep sense of responsibility. He recognizes what Gene Getz refers to as the first of seven key principles of evangelism. "First, *every local body of believers must be responsible for its own community.* It is responsible to saturate that community with *love* and to demonstrate a *unity* and *oneness* that provide the basis for verbal communication; to demonstrate a Christian life style in all human relationships, so as to create a basis on which to discuss the life-changing Christ" (italics his).[22] Paul takes responsibility for the community of faith in Rome. Although he had not pioneered the church there, he desired to stabilize it. He uses the gospel to accomplish this task.

Paul pens a personal letter to the Christians in Rome on the fulcrum of the gospel message. "For I am not ashamed of the gospel, for it is the power of God to salvation to all who are believing, to Jews first but also to Greeks."[23] He uses the gospel to balance the tenuous relationship between the Jewish and Gentile Christians in Rome. The gospel represents the one element on which both parties should agree. Paul invests in this one commonality because he understands its universal resolution and application. The gospel furnishes Paul the cohesion he needs to solidify the Christians in Rome.

Paul recognizes the eschatological influence and impact of the gospel that he has preached for two decades. He concedes its eschatological significance in his concluding remarks to the saints at Rome. Paul summarizes his mission by acknowledging, "that from Jerusalem and in a circular manner as far as Illyricum I have fulfilled the gospel of Christ."[24] Conn and Ortiz alert their readers to the incorrect translation of this verse in many Bible versions.

Favored English translations (KJV, NKJV, NIV) render this 'I have fully preached,' which may give the mistaken impression that he is reflecting on the fullness with which he set forth the gospel(cf. Acts 20:20, 27). The Jerusalem Bible translates it 'I have preached the Good News to the utmost of my capacity,' underlining the strenuous efforts of the apostle. All these translations miss the link between the apostle's commission that he expounds here and the sense of completeness that he now expresses. Behind the language is, again, Paul's sense of the place of world mission in the history redemption. In his ministry to Jews and Gentiles he saw the triumph of the Lord as peoples 'from Jerusalem all the way around to Illyricum' found their way to God in Christ. The eschatological expectations of the ingathering of the Gentiles had become eschatological experiences in the mission of Paul.[25]

Paul deems the Church, which consists of Jews and Gentiles, as fulfillment of Isaiah's prophecies, especially chapters 49-66, and his own ministry as allied with this realization of the eschatological age. Consequently, he unveils the correlation between the eschaton of Isaiah and the gospel that he espouses.

When Paul invests in the gospel of Jesus Christ he is investing in the word of God "which will not (and cannot) return to God void."[26] Concurrently, like the aqueducts of Rome, the city becomes a conduit through which this gospel travels. "If we penetrate cities, the gospel will travel. Large cities are both *magnets*, drawing the nations into them, and *magnifiers*, broadcasting the gospel out into the hinterlands (italics his)."[27] Paul envisions Rome and the gospel respectively as his *magnet* and *magnifier*. Yet, he understands that humans provide the best channels through which may flow the gospel message. Accordingly, he invests in the people, Christian Jews and Gentiles, of Rome.

One might argue that Paul actually reinvests in the Christians at Rome, at least some of them. Upon close inspection of his greetings in 16:3-16, one notes that Paul knows well many of the leaders and workers in the churches at Rome. He greets twenty-six individuals by name as well as other unidentified sisters, brothers, and church members. This list may have provided the entire church there with references for Paul, or it may have been one mode of demonstrating unity among the Jewish and Gentile contingency. This writer opines that Paul has both consequences in mind. This select group served as "Green Eyes" for Paul and "enabled (Paul) to earn the right to present the gospel."[28] These people offered Paul an advantage in Rome and its churches as well as granted him access to both groups of believers. "It also importantly reflects the mixed Jewish and Gentile character of the congregation."[29] Paul invests in Jewish and Gentile Christians; subsequently, he invests in both factions. This investment, like the City of Rome and the Gospel, necessitates risks and generates benefits for Paul and his eschatological mission.

What are the risks and benefits for the apostle? Investments have a propensity of low risk, medium risk, or high risk. Typically, the higher the risk the greater the return or benefit. When dealing with cities, the gospel, and people, the risk factors are better defined as high, higher, and highest!; this approach of investing in the city, the gospel, and people yields excellent benefits but at much greater risks. Still, the gospel challenges the Church to take these risks. This is the clarion call of urban ministers and ministries: "The Body of Christ must be risk takers!"[30]

Paul champions this principle of risk taking in his theology and exemplifies it in his letter to the Roman Christians. Paul endangers his life by journeying to Rome where the city suspects those who call themselves "Christian." Paul jeopardizes his comprehension of eschatology as delineated in the Hebrew Scriptures and demarcated in his "gospel." For example, how will the Jewish and Gentile Christians construe, identify with, and value the eschatological vision of Paul as he presents it in chapters two and three as well as nine through eleven? He imperils his missionary goal of reaching Spain by investing in different ethnic groups in the Roman churches. He states explicitly in 15:24 that he anticipates being sent to Spain by the Roman churches. Paul is investing in the churches at Rome, and he expects them to invest correspondingly in his mission. Paul communicates these risks by expounding the mutual benefits.

What advantages do the city, the gospel, and the people of Rome offer? What benefits does Paul offer? The city is a microcosm of the nations. "If a city is anything, at least in ideological form, it is an organic, dynamic series of relationships, interwoven in a common crucible."[31] This description by Bakke references Jerusalem, particularly the New Jerusalem of Revelation 21-22, but I am persuaded that it is also a paradigm of what cities can and should be when the Church saturates them with salt and light. "The record in Acts and the epistles of the total impact of the church on the world is clear.... Christians helped to change the total culture. They affected and infected the total community." [32] These cultural consequences signify the eschatological city in which Paul invests. He perceives that Rome is advancing toward this ideal. "First, I thank my God through Jesus Christ concerning all of you, since your faith is being propagated throughout the whole world."[33] Therefore, he desires to visit Rome while passing through toward Spain, the periphery of the empire. His eschatological vision allows him *insight* into the city of Rome and *far sight* to the cities on the outskirts of the empire. The eyes of Paul converge on every large city between Rome and Spain!

The ability of Paul to see beyond Rome derives from his understanding of the benefits of the gospel. One cannot overemphasize the place – the city itself. "God's kingdom agenda seeks the personal salvation of all persons and the social transformation of all places."[34] The gospel is potent and universal. Paul insists, "it is the power of God for salvation to all who are believing, to Jews first, but also to Greeks."[35] It is effective as well as comprehensive, profitable in addition to beneficial, liberating and, at the same time, obligatory. The gospel orients one to the places and the peoples beckoning for preservation and illumination, for salt and light. The ears of Paul (as keen as his eyes) hear the dirge of the individual among the laments of the populace. He realizes that one must invest in people in order to acquire the city.

People typify the highest risk for investment; however, they also exemplify the highest yield. Paul learned this lesson early in his ministry with regard to John Mark. (Compare Acts 15:36-41 with 2 Timothy 4:11.) God risked God's very best for humanity. If God reasons that people are worth dying for, then the Church must deem them worthy of investment. God gave God's paramount investment with the highest risk for the greatest benefit! The gospel offers the Church the firm basis for investing in people.

The people of the city offer diversity, the very substance that God uses to formulate and unify His kingdom. In first century, Greco-Roman society "the cities welcomed aliens (*metics*) providing they had a citizen sponsor. They brought fresh ideas, new ways, beneficial skills, and an eagerness to work – all valuable commodities for the city in need of economic stimulation and constant renewal."[36] Paul affirms this diversity in his list of colleagues in Romans 16. The names include Jews, Greeks, and even (former) pagans. The list unveils civic leaders as well as slaves. Additionally, one should note the benefits from this group: some had risked themselves for Paul; others had endured imprisonment with Paul; another ministered to him as a "spiritual mother!" Relationships are essential. Fuder identifies "relationship as one of the four distinct stages of preparation for living and ministering in a city."[37] The risks are high; the advantages, beneficial. People may or may not yield temporal benefits, but they always yield eternal benefits. Paul appreciates and accentuates this principle. Sequentially, one acknowledges how Paul, the ancient city of Rome, and *The Letter of Romans* offer contemporary society a paradigm of philosophical and theological bases as well as identify pragmatic challenges (risks) and beneficial solutions for investing in the city.

Paul and his letter to the churches in Rome identify methods of investments such as the city itself, the gospel, and the people. The apostle and his message present various techniques of investment that include utilizing the existent diversity in order to engage and unify the body of Christ. Paul implemented the principle that "the local city church staff should increasingly match the ethnicity, class, and culture of the church's members."[38] Paul denotes the risk or risks encountered through this type of investment, and, at the same time, he reveals the many benefits from such an investment. Through his correspondence, Paul illustrates how the Church, the body of Christ, might contribute to this investment.

This writer surmises that this ancient letter can and does serve as a contemporary paradigm for investment opportunities of the magnitude needed in our cities. However, one must be careful not to view the city, the gospel, or the people as objects to manipulate for personal gain. This writer does not intend the word "benefit" in this way. Rome, the gospel, and the people are not objects for Paul; they are opportunities. They represent not problems but possibilities.

Paul emphasizes the church *for the sake of* the city, not the church *instead of* the city. Neither Church ministries nor civic leadership can "run programs and services for the city from the safety of the suburbs, substituting technology for building relationships in the neighborhood."[39]

One must advance the city, the gospel, and the people through infrastructural renovation, spiritual transformation, and interpersonal communication. These actions require the most diverse investments, entail the greatest risks, and provide the highest yields; these are eternal which pervades the temporal.

Notes

1. Advertisement heard by this author on November 20, 2007 on the WKMG Radio (Magic 104.1 FM).

2. Ray Bakke, *A Theology as Big as the City* (Downers Grove, IL: InterVarsity Press, 1997), 34.

3. *The Zondervan Pictorial Encyclopedia of the Bible*, s.v. "Rome."

4. Henry C. Boren, *Roman Society: A Social, Economic, and Cultural History* (Lexington, MA: D.C. Heath and Company, 1977), 178.

5. Ibid., 179.

6. Ibid., 180.

7. Suetonius, *The Twelve Caesars*, trans. J.C. Rolfe (Boston: Harvard University Press, 1998), 25.4.

8. Udo Schnelle, *Apostle Paul: His Life and Theology*, trans. M. Eugene Boring (Grand Rapids, MI: Baker Academic, 2005), 303.

9. Unless indicated otherwise, all New Testament passages are the translation of this author from Eberhard Nestle and Kurt Aland, ed., *Novum Testamentum Graece*, 27th ed. (Stuttgart: Deutsche Bibelgesellschaft, 1993), 375.

10. Ibid., 380.

11. Bakke, *A Theology as Big as the City*, 131.

12. Rodney Stark, *Cities of God: The Real Story of How Christianity Became an Urban Movement and Conquered Rome* (San Francisco: HarperCollins Publishers, 2006), 132.

13. Ibid., 237-238.

14. Harvie M. Conn and Manuel Ortiz, *Urban Ministry: The Kingdom, the City, and the People of God* (Downers Grove, IL: InterVarsity Press, 2001), 127ff.

15. Joseph Shulam, *A Commentary on the Jewish Roots of Romans* (Baltimore, MD: Messianic Jewish Publishers, 1997), 14.

16. Author's translation of Romans 1:11-13 from *Novum Testamentum Graece*, 409.

17. Author's translation of Romans 15:24 from *Novum Testamentum Graece*, 437.

18. Conn and Ortiz, *Urban Ministry*, 138.

19. Author's translation of Acts 18:11 from *Novum Testamentum Graece*, 376.

20. Author's translation of Acts 19:10 from *Novum Testamentum Graece*, 379.

21. Calvin J. Roetzel, *The World that Shaped the New Testament* (Atlanta: John Knox Press, 1985), 72.

22. Gene A. Getz, *Sharpening the Focus of the Church* (Chicago: Moody Press, 1974), 40.

23. Author's translation of Romans 1:16 from *Novum Testamentum Graece*, 410.

24. Author's translation of Romans 15:19c from *Novum Testamentum Graece*, 437.

25. Conn and Ortiz, *Urban Ministry*, 139 and 140.

26. Isaiah 55:11, NASB.

27. Bakke, *A Theology as Big as the City*, 168.

28. John Fuder, ed., *A Heart for the City: Effective Ministries to the Urban Community* (Chicago: Moody Publishers, 1999), 111, 116.

29. Shulam, *A Commentary on the Jewish Roots of Romans*, 513.

30. John Fuder, Class notes, August 9, 2007. This call still reverberates in my ears and permeates in my heart.

31. Bakke, *A Theology as Big as the City*, 63.

32. Getz, *Sharpening the Focus of the Church*, 73.

33. Author's translation of Romans 1:8 from *Novum Testamentum Graece*, 409.

34. Bakke, *A Theology as Big as the City*, 66.

35. Author's translation of Romans 1:16b from *Novum Testamentum Graece*, 410.

36. Roetzel, *The World that Shaped the New Testament*, 70.

37. John Fuder, Handout, "*How to Reach A City for Christ*," August 10, 2007.

38. Bakke, *A Theology as Big as the City*, 146.

39. Fuder, ed., *A Heart for the City*, 34.

Bibliography

Bakke, Ray. *A Theology as Big as the City*. Downers Grove,   IL: InterVarsity Press, 1997.

Boren, Henry C. *Roman Society: A Social, Economic, and Cultural History*. Lexington, MA: D.C. Heath and Company, 1977.

Conn, Harvie M. and Manuel Ortiz. *Urban Ministry: The Kingdom, the City, and the People of God*. Downers Grove, IL: InterVarsity Press, 2001.

Fuder, John, ed. *A Heart for the City: Effective Ministries to the Urban Community*. Chicago: Moody Publishers, 1999.

Getz, Gene A. *Sharpening the Focus of the Church*. Chicago: Moody Press, 1974.

Nestle, Ebehard and Kurt Aland, ed., *Novum Testamentum Graece*, 27th ed. Stuttgart: Deutsche Bibelgesellschaft, 1993.

Roetzel, Calvin J. *The World That Shaped the New Testament*. Atlanta: John Knox Press, 1985.

Shulam, Joseph with Hilary Le Cornu. *A Commentary on the Jewish Roots of Romans*. Baltimore, MD: Messianic Jewish Publishers, 1997.

Schnelle, Udo. *Apostle Paul: His Life and Theology*. Translated by M. Eugene Boring. Grand Rapids, MI: Baker Academic, 2005.

Stark, Rodney. *Cities of God: The Real Story of How Christianity Became an Urban Movement and Conquered Rome*. San Francisco: HarperCollins Publishers, 2006.

Suetonius, *The Twelve Caesars*, vol. II. Translated by J.C. Rolfe. Boston: Harvard University Press, 1998.

Tenney, Merrill C., ed. *The Zondervan Pictorial Encyclopedia of the Bible*, vol. 5. Grand Rapids, MI: Zondervan Publishing House, 1975, 1976.

BY FAITH WE UNDERSTAND

BY
IRENE BELYEU
AUTHOR

ABSTRACT

Even as the Christians of the New Testament era were sometimes called "ignorant and unlearned men," so the worldly-wise of our modern culture sometimes contemptuously label Christians. The apostle Paul was a highly educated man, yet, after meeting Christ, he scorned his worldly-wisdom in comparison to the knowledge of God. The Bible declares the Wisdom of God as the very agent of creation, the most desirable attribute for quality of life, and the ultimate fulfillment of eternal life. This faith in God adds the dimension of His loving purpose to every discipline of learning.

In the early days of the Pentecostal movement, there was a strong current of anti-intellectualism among the laity. Some evidence of this was the substitution of the word *cemetery* for the word *seminary*, suggesting that those who had gone through seminary were lifeless. It was commonly said that they were "educated beyond their reach." Alternatively, that "oppositions of science falsely so-called" had spoiled them.

It does seem that there was some correlation between the occurrence of signs and wonders in *"unlearned and ignorant men"* and the lack thereof in those more learned. Why? Should we then glorify ignorance? Even in New Testament times, the Pharisees were considered the "intelligentsia" and Paul was one of them until he met Christ on the road to Damascus. After that, he knew that only the knowledge of Christ was valuable; all else was but dung:

(7) But what things were gain to me, those I counted loss for Christ. (8) Yea doubtless, and I count all things but loss for the excellency of the knowledge of Christ Jesus my Lord: for whom I have suffered the loss of all things, and do count them but dung, that I may win Christ. (9) And be found in him, not having mine own righteousness, which is of the law, but that which is through the faith of

Christ, the righteousness which is of God by faith. (10) That I may know him, and the power of his resurrection, and the fellowship of his sufferings, being made conformable unto his death. Philippians 3:7-11[78]

THE QUESTION

The burning question then becomes: "Is it possible to merge faith with learning without losing the power of the Holy Spirit in signs and wonders?" Are the two mutually exclusive?

We know from the Biblical injunctions that we are commanded to seek Wisdom: *"Wisdom is the principal thing; therefore get wisdom: and with all thy getting, get understanding."* A large portion of the Bible is Wisdom Literature: Proverbs, Ecclesiastes, Job, Psalms 19, 37, 104, 107, 147, 148 and many other short passages in the Old Testament. In the New Testament, we should list the Book of James as one of the finest examples of Wisdom Literature.[79] These are a very valuable part of the Word of God:

---

[78] Spelling and punctuation of quotations from the King James Version are those of the text itself.

[79] Zondervan Pictorial Bible Dictionary, General Editor, Merrill C. Tenney. Zondervan Publishing House, Grand Rapids, Michigan. 1967. "Wisdom," p. 895.

All scripture is given by inspiration of God, and is profitable for doctrine, for reproof, for correction, for instruction in righteousness: that the man of God may be perfect, thoroughly furnished unto all good works. 2Timothy 3:16-17

We know, then, that to gain wisdom through learning is not the problem, but rather the answer. Surely, we are warned that there are teachings called *science* that *are* falsely so-called. However, we must not reject all that is called *science* because some are false. We should learn to discern the difference. True science is always compatible with God's Truth.

THE ANSWER

If higher learning is not the problem, then what is? The problem is pride – being *"puffed up"*:

Knowledge puffeth up, but charity edifieth. And if any man think that he knoweth any thing, he knoweth nothing yet as he ought to know. But if any man love God, the same is known of him. 1Corinthians 8:1b-3

The solution is found in Hebrews 11:3:

Through faith we understand that the worlds were framed by the word of God, so that things which are seen were not made of things which do appear."

The word *understand*, literally means "to stand under," as a foundation. Webster gives one definition as: "To accept as established or laid down as a condition... to assume as conditions expressed or understood." In logical terms, it means *axiomatic*, a statement of a self-evident truth; an established principle that is universally received. In other words, it is something we assume to be true, an *assumption*. This basic truth is assumed true by faith in something. By faith in God, we assume, or understand, that: *"In the beginning God created the heavens and the earth,"* as stated in Genesis chapter 1. This was accomplished by His Word, which is Wisdom, which is Christ. God is a Spirit. So behind every physical and natural discipline is the truth that it was originally created by the Spirit.

Without faith in God, learning does not lead to truth: 2 Timothy 3:7: *"Ever learning and never able to come to the knowledge of the Truth."* Understanding the spiritual origin of creation, then, underlies all consequent physical or spiritual information, knowledge, or learning in any science, philosophy, art, technology, psychology, geology, astronomy, cartography or any principality or power. It is the basis for all wisdom and spiritual understanding:

(12) Giving thanks unto the Father, which hath made us meet to be partakers of the inheritance of the saints in light: (13) Who hath delivered us from the power of darkness, and hath translated us into the kingdom of his dear Son: (14) In whom we have redemption through his blood, even the forgiveness of sins: (15) Who is the image of the invisible God, the firstborn of every creature: (16) For by him were all things created, that are in heaven, and that are in earth, visible and invisible, whether they be thrones, or dominions, or principalities, or powers: all things were created by him and for him. Colossians 1:12-16.

The creation was by and for Jesus to give Him the preeminence in His kingdom:

(17) And he is before all things, and by him all things consist. (18) And he is the head of the body, the church: who is the beginning, the firstborn from the dead; that in all things he might have the preeminence, (19) For it pleased the Father that in him should all fullness dwell; (20) And, having made peace through the blood of his cross, by him to reconcile all things unto himself; by him, I say, whether they be things in earth, or things in heaven. Colossians 1:12-20.

Thou art worthy, O Lord, to receive glory and honour and power: for thou hast created all things, and for thy pleasure they are and were created. Revelation 4:11

The truth of the divine Creator and his creation is the basis for all further learning. It is the unifying factor that reconciles all truth; in Jesus all things *consist*, that is, hold together.

Proverbs 9:10: "*The fear of the Lord is the beginning of wisdom: and the knowledge of the holy is understanding.*"

Wisdom is understanding: Proverbs 8:14: "*Counsel is mine and sound wisdom: I am understanding, I have strength.*"

Wisdom was born before the Creation, and the natural, physical world was made by Wisdom. In Proverbs 18:22-32 Wisdom is speaking:

(22) The Lord possessed me in the beginning of his way, before the works of old, (23) I was set up from everlasting, from the beginning, or ever the earth was. (24) When there were no depths I was brought forth; when there were no fountains abounding with water. (25) Before the mountains were settled, before the hills was I brought forth: (26) While as yet he had not made the earth, nor the fields, nor the highest part of the dust of the world. (27) When he prepared the heavens I was there; when he set a compass on the face of the depth:

(28) When he established the clouds above: when he strengthened the fountains of the deep: (29) When he gave to the sea his decree that the waters should not pass his commandment: when he appointed the foundations of the earth: (30) Then I was by him, as one brought up with him: and I was daily his delight, rejoicing always before him; (31) Rejoicing in the habitable part of his earth; and my delights were with the sons of men. (32) Now therefore hearken unto me, O ye children: for blessed are they that keep my ways.

This original Wisdom is Christ, Colossians 1:15-17 as quoted above. Jesus has been made Wisdom for us, 1Corinthians 1:22-24, 30.

WHAT IS WISDOM?

The Bible speaks of two kinds of wisdom, the wisdom of this world and the wisdom of God. One may be learned in the wisdom of the world, yet a fool: *"The fool has said in his heart 'There is no God,'"* Psalm 14:1; 53:1. This scripture might well serve as the definition of a fool. If one believes there is no God, then there is no intelligent Creator, but all exists by some blind, amoral accident. He has no basic axiom upon which to base his reasoning.

The wisdom literature of the Bible clearly spells out the positive benefits of wisdom, as well as the negative consequences of refusing to accept wisdom's call. The Book of Proverbs begins with:

(1)The proverbs of Solomon the son of David, king of Israel; (2)To know wisdom and instruction; to perceive the words of understanding; (3)To receive the instruction of wisdom, justice, and judgment, and equity;(4)To give subtlety to the simple, to the young man knowledge and discretion. Proverbs 1:1-4

The Book of Ecclesiastes sums up the whole matter:

Let us hear the conclusion of the whole matter: Fear God and keep his commandments: for this is the whole duty of man.(14)For God shall bring every work into judgment, with every secret thing, whether it be good, or whether it be evil. Ecclesiastes 12:13-14

The Book of James is a book of wisdom:

(1:5) If any of you lack wisdom, let him ask of God, that giveth to all men liberally, and upbraideth not; and it shall be given him.

However, this wisdom comes only with faith:

(1:6) But let him ask in faith, nothing wavering. For he that wavereth is like a wave of the sea, driven with the wind and tossed.

(7)For let not that man think that he shall receive anything of the Lord. (8)A double minded man is unstable in all his ways.

This wisdom is not available for selfish indulgence:

(4:1-3)From whence come wars and fightings among you? Come they not hence even of your lusts that war in your members? (2)Ye lust and have not: ye kill, and desire to have, and cannot obtain: ye fight and war, yet ye have not, because ye ask not. (3)Ye ask, and receive not, because ye ask amiss, that ye may consume it upon your lusts.

Ultimately, Jesus is incarnate Wisdom:

17) For Christ sent me not to baptize, but to preach the gospel: not with wisdom of words, lest the cross of Christ should be made of none effect. (18) For the preaching of the cross is to them that perish foolishness; but unto us which are saved it is the power of God. (19) For it is written, I will destroy the wisdom of the wise, and will bring to nothing the understanding of the prudent.

(20) For after that in the wisdom of God the world by wisdom knew not God, it pleased God by the foolishness of preaching to save them that believe. (21) For after that in the wisdom of God the world by wisdom knew not God, it pleased God by the foolishness of preaching to save them that believe.

(22) For the Jews require a sign and the Greeks seek after wisdom: (23) But we preach Christ crucified, unto the Jews a stumblingblock, and unto the Greeks foolishness; (24) But unto them which are called, both Jews and Greeks, Christ the power of God, and the wisdom of God. (25) Because the foolishness of God is wiser than men; and the weakness of God is stronger than men.

(26) For ye see our calling, brethren, how that not many wise men after the flesh, not many mighty, not many noble, are called: (27) But God hath chosen the foolish things of the world to confound the wise; and God hath chosen the weak things of the world to confound the things which are mighty; (28) And base things of the world, and things which are despised, hath God chosen, yea, and things which are not, to bring to nought things that are: (29) That no flesh should glory in his presence.

(30) But of him are ye in Christ Jesus, who of God is made unto us wisdom, and righteousness, and sanctification, and redemption: (31) That, according as it is written, He that glorieth, let him glory in the Lord. 1 Corinthians 1:17-31.

<u>The Wisdom of God: Revelation</u>

However, what is the wisdom of God? Is it religious ritual and conformity to cultural traditions and legal edicts? The wisdom of God, knowing the Creator, is as far above worldly wisdom as scriptural holiness is above mere morality. While these things may be a part of it, they fall far short of its essence, for the wisdom of God is *manifold*, that is, it is many faceted, Ephesians 3:10. It is many-sided, with innumerable aspects. It includes the intellect of logic and reasoning as well as spiritual insight into divine mysteries. "*Wisdom dwells with prudence* [subtlety] *and finds out the knowledge of witty inventions*, Proverbs 8:12. That is, wisdom is the source of creativity and working knowledge.

However, *faith* does not come by reason but by revelation. *Revelation* gives us the ability to *see* a *mystery*.

(16)And Simon Peter answered and said, Thou art the Christ, the Son of the living God. (17)And Jesus answered and said unto him, Blessed art thou, Simon Barjona: for flesh and blood hath not revealed it unto thee, but my Father which is in heaven. Matthew 16:16-17

The wisdom of God goes beyond mere intellect to give us spiritual insight, *revelation* of the mysteries, unattainable by our fleshly endeavors:

(3) How that by revelation he made known unto me the mystery: (as I wrote afore in few words, (4) Whereby, when ye read, ye may understand my knowledge in the mystery of Christ) (5) Which in other ages was not made known unto the sons of men, as it is now revealed unto his holy apostles and prophets by the Spirit; (6) That the Gentiles should be fellowheirs, and of the same body, and partakers of his

promise in Christ by the gospel: (7) Whereof I was made a minister, according to the gift of the grace of God given unto me by the effectual working of his power.

(8) Unto me, who am less that the least of all saints, is this grace given, that I should preach among the Gentiles the unsearchable riches of Christ; (9) And to make all men see what is the fellowship of the mystery, which from the beginning of the world hath been hid in God, who created all things by Jesus Christ: (10) To the intent that now unto the principalities and powers in heavenly places might be known by the Church the manifold wisdom of God, (11) According to the eternal purpose which he purposed in Christ Jesus our Lord: (12) In whom we have boldness of access with confidence by the faith of him.

(13) Wherefore I desire that ye faint not at my tribulations for you, which is your glory (14) For this cause I bow my knees unto the Father of our Lord Jesus Christ, (15) Of whom the whole family in heaven and earth is named, (16) That he would grant you, according to the riches of his glory, to be strengthened with might by his Spirit in the inner man; (17) That Christ may dwell in your hearts by faith; that ye, being rooted and grounded in love, (18) May be able to comprehend with all saints what is the breadth, and length, and depth, and height; (19) And to know the love of Christ, which passeth knowledge, that ye might be filled with all the fullness of God. (Ephesians 3:3-19)

Note that: (1) Paul received this knowledge of the *mystery* by *revelation*, not through the intellect; (2) That the *mystery* had been hidden in the creation which God created by Jesus Christ; (3) That God's purpose was that the knowledge be revealed to Paul so that it would be revealed *through* Paul to the Church so that *through* the Church, in turn, it might be revealed to the principalities and powers in the spiritual realms; and (4) That being rooted and grounded in love gives the ability to *comprehend* the love of Christ. Moreover, with Christ in their hearts, the Church might be able to *know* the otherwise *unknowable* love of God!

What a statement of the role of revelation in merging faith and learning!

The Wisdom of God: Light

Learning requires insight, understanding. Repetition of forms or phrases without meaning is mere ritual, rote. When real insight occurs, it is as if the faculty of sight is activated. It is sometimes expressed as "the *Aha* moment." Often we hear the phrase: "I see" to express our understanding or comprehension of a thing. It is sometimes expressed as "having the light," or the light *dawning*, on any certain subject.

Seeing requires light. Light, in the Scriptures, is of a threefold nature: First, the literal light that gives sight to the eyes, revealing physical things; secondly, the light of understanding, giving intellectual knowledge; thirdly, the light of spiritual revelation. By the light of the eyes, man is oriented to his natural surroundings; by the light of understanding, he may know abstractions such as truth and beauty; by the light of spiritual revelation, he may know God. We do not fully know a thing until we have the spiritual revelation of it, Gods will and purpose for it. This is where faith *must* merge with learning.

Eye hath not seen, nor ear heard, neither have entered the heart of Man the things which God hath prepared for them that love Him. But God hath revealed them unto us by His Spirit: for the Spirit searcheth all things, yea, the deep things of God. 1 Corinthians 2:9

Literal light requires natural eyesight; the light of understanding requires access to the means of illumination usually by the aid of a teacher or mentor; spiritual light requires the mediation of the Holy Ghost Who will "*lead you into all truth.*" Literal meaning may be received by any capable of reading or hearing; understanding and perception of truth may be received by those capable of translating symbols; but spiritual revelation comes only through a peculiar and particular relationship and orientation between God and Man.

God is ever manifest, revealed, in Light:

(1)*That which was from the beginning, which we have heard, which we have seen with our eyes, which we have looked upon, and our hands have handled, of the Word of Life; (2) (For the Life was manifested,* [revealed, brought to light], *and we have seen it, and bear witness, and show unto you that Eternal Life, which was with the Father, and was manifested unto us:)... (5)This then is the message which we have heard of Him, and declare unto you, that God is Light, and in Him is no darkness at all."* 1 John 1:1, 2, 5

Every good gift and every perfect gift is from above, and cometh down from the Father of Lights, with whom is no variableness, neither shadow of turning. James 1:17

(14b) Until the appearing [revelation] *of our Lord Jesus Christ: (15) Which in His times He shall shew* [reveal], *Who is the blessed and only Potentate, the King of kings, and Lord of lords; (16) Who only hath immortality, dwelling in the Light which no man can approach unto; whom no man hath seen, nor can see; to Whom be honour and power everlasting. Amen.* 1 Tim. 6:14b-16

While God is *unapproachable* Light, Christ is *revealed* light. Jesus is The Light of the World:

Then spake Jesus again unto them, saying, I am the light of the world: he that followeth me shall not walk in darkness but shall have the light of life. John 8:12

As long as I am in the world I am the light of the world. John 9:5

(35) Then Jesus said unto them. Yet a little while is the Light with you. Walk while ye have the Light, lest darkness come upon you: for he that walketh in darkness knoweth not whither he goeth. (36) While ye have Light, believe in the Light, that ye may be the children of Light. These things spake Jesus, and departed, and did hide Himself from them. John 12:35-6

We, His people, are the bearers of His Light:

(14)Ye are the light of the world. A city that is set on an hill cannot be hid…. (16)Let your light so shine before men, that they may see your good works, and glorify your Father which is in heaven. Matthew 5:14, 16

We are in the Kingdom of Light:

Who hath delivered us from the power of darkness, and hath translated us into the kingdom of His dear Son. Colossians 1:13

The book of Beginnings, Genesis, starts with the revelation of the Secret of Light:

(1)In the beginning God created the heavens and the earth. (2)And the earth was without form, and void; And darkness was upon the face of the deep. And the Spirit of God moved upon the face of the waters. (3) And God said, Let there be Light: and there was Light. Genesis 1:1-3

The Gospel of John starts from this same beginning point:

(1)In the beginning was the Word, and the Word was with God, and the Word was God. (2) The same was in the beginning with God. (3) All things were made by Him; and without Him was not anything made that was made. (4) In Him was Life: and the Life was the Light of men. (5) And the Light shineth in darkness; and the darkness comprehended it not. (6) There was a man sent from God whose name was John. (7) The same came for a witness, to bear witness of the Light, that all men through Him might believe. (8) He was not that Light, but was sent to bear witness of that Light. (9) That was the true Light which lighteth every man that cometh into the world. (10)He was in the world, and the world was made by him, and the world knew Him not. (11) He came unto His own, and His own received Him not. (12) But as many as received Him, to them gave He power to become sons of God, even to them that believe on His name: (13) Which were

born, not of blood, nor of the will of the flesh, nor of the will of man, but of God. (14) And the Word was made Flesh, and dwelt among us, (And we beheld His glory, [beautiful Light], *the glory as of the only begotten of the Father,) full of grace and truth.* John 1:1-14

The prophet Isaiah saw this beautiful truth:

(1b) The Lord called me from the womb, from the body of my mother he named my name.... (5) And now saith the Lord, who formed me from the womb to be his servant, to bring Jacob back to him, and that Israel might be gathered to him.... (6)And he said, "It is a light thing that thou shouldest be my servant to raise up the tribes of Jacob and to restore the preserved of Israel; I will give thee as a light to the Gentiles, that thou mayest be my salvation unto the end of the earth." Isaiah 49:1b, 5-6. See also Isaiah 44:24.

The purpose of Light, or Revelation, is *to show,* (cause to see), the way of salvation. Learning without the purpose of God's love is meaningless and worthless, 1Corinthians 13:2.

Except in the Spirit, we must now see Christ in symbols for we are under the veil, which is our flesh.

For now we see through a glass darkly, but then face to face: now, I know in part, but then shall I know even as also I am known. (1 Cor. 13:12)

The fact cannot be overemphasized that God is a Spirit and therefore cannot be confined to any form. When God revealed Himself in a visible form, according to the Scriptures, He revealed Himself in mediums of Light which, while visible, could never be taken as an idol-form neither could it be made by the works of men's hands. We may safely say that God is always revealed in some form of light and there is no other *visible* form in which He has revealed Himself.

Before sin brought about the necessity of the veil, God walked with Adam in an open way, but afterwards He only revealed His Light, or His "glory," which might also be interpreted His garment. Repeatedly we are told that no man hath seen God. Moses prayed: "*I beseech thee, shew me thy glory*," (Exod. 34:18), for he was afraid to "see God" for it meant certain death. How marvelous it is when God breaks through the veil of our doubting flesh to show us His glory. This Christ did in His incarnation, for He is "*the brightness of His glory, and the express image of His person.*" Hebrews 1:3

The Light that God commanded to be conceived or began in the beginning waxed brighter and brighter throughout the revealed Scriptures. However, while this Light was *conceived* in the Old Testament, it was at that time hidden, but in the incarnation, it was revealed, and in the

Spirit, it is perfected. *"For God so loved the world that He gave His only begotten Son."*

LIGHT!

<u>Wisdom Is A Tree of Life:</u>

(18) She [Wisdom] *is a tree of life to them that lay hold upon her: and happy is every one that retaineth her. (19) The Lord by wisdom hath founded the earth; by understanding hath he established the heaven. (20) By his knowledge the depths are broken up, and the clouds drop down the dew.* Proverbs 3:18-20

We know that in the Garden of Eden, the Tree of the Knowledge of Good and Evil was the only tree that they were forbidden to eat of. They were cast out of the Garden because they had eaten of that tree. Yet, because of their sinful condition, God reserved their right to eat of the Tree of Life, *"lest he put forth his hand, and take also of the tree of life, and eat, and live forever."* In mercy, God did not allow humanity to live forever in their sinful, fallen state. The Tree of Life was to be reserved for Jesus and those who would come to God through Him:

(7) He that hath an ear, let him hear what the Spirit saith unto the churches; To him that overcometh will I give to eat of the tree of life, which is in the midst of the paradise of God. Revelation 2:7

(2) And in the midst of the street of it, and on either side of the river, was there the tree of life, which bare twelve manner of fruits, and yielded her fruit every month: and the leaves of the tree were for the healing of the nations... (14) Blessed are they that do his commandments, that they may have right to the tree of life, and may enter in through the gates into the city. Revelation 22:2, 14

Therefore, Wisdom is no small gift, but greatly to be desired, giving happiness in this present world and eternal life in the Paradise of God. But how do we partake of this tree in the here and now? Proverbs chapter 15 gives the rationale for the careful use of the tongue and the power of our words:

(1)A soft answer turneth away wrath: but grievous words stir up anger. (2) The tongue of the wise useth knowledge aright: but the mouth of fools poureth out foolishness. (3) The eyes of the Lord are in every place, beholding the evil and the good. (4) A wholesome tongue is a tree of life: but perverseness therein is a breach in the spirit. Proverbs 15:1-4

1. The word translated *wholesome* here means "healing, a curative, a medicine." This

leads us to Jesus' teachings concerning the power of our words.

2.

3. <u>The Creative Word of Wisdom</u>

4.

5. Must we be "ignorant and unlearned men," in order to do signs and wonders? Certainly not, but our wisdom must be merged with the faith of God.

6. Just as faith in the truth that God created the heavens and the earth by His spoken Word, by faith in the Word of God in our mouths, we create the signs and wonders promised by our Lord and Savior, Jesus Christ. Perhaps the most comprehensive expression of this promise is found in John 14:12-14:

7. *Verily, verily, I say unto you, He that believeth on me, the works that I do shall he do also; and greater works than these shall he do; because I go unto my Father. (13) And whatsoever ye shall ask in my name, that will I do, that the Father may be glorified in the*

Son. (14) If ye shall ask any thing in my name, I will do it.

8. Why did he say: *"Because I go unto my Father"*? Verse 24 explains this: *"The word which ye hear is not mine, but the Father's which sent me."* The word in Jesus' mouth was the word of God the Father that created the heavens and the earth. Jesus had previously said, John 6:63: *"The words that I speak unto you, they are spirit, and they are life."* God's word is not idle or vain, but virile, potent, accomplishing His purposes, Isaiah 55:11. It is the "Word of Life," John 1:4 and Philippians 2:16. The Word of God is living:

9. *For the word, that God speaks is alive and full of power [making it active, operative, energizing, and effective.* Hebrews 4:12 AMP [See also Luke 4:32: *His word was with power."*]

10.   In his prayer to the Father in John 17:8 Jesus says:

11.   *I have given them the words which thou gavest me; and they have received them, and have known surely that I came out from thee, and they have believed that thou didst send me.* John 17:8

12. Again, in verse 14 of that chapter he prays: "*I have given them thy word.*"

13. What were the works of Jesus that He said believers, those who have faith in Him, should do? In Matthew 8:16 He: "*Cast out spirits with his word and healed all that were sick.*"

14. In Matthew 17:20 after healing a child of seizures He says:

15. *If ye have faith as a grain of mustard seed, ye shall say unto this mountain, Remove hence to yonder place; and it shall remove; and nothing shall be impossible unto you*"

16. In Matthew 21:21-22 He caused the fig tree to wither and promised:

17. *(21) If ye have faith, and doubt not, ye shall not only do this which is done to the fig tree, but also if ye shall say unto this mountain, Be thou removed, and be thou cast into the sea; it shall be done. (22) And all things, whatsoever ye shall ask in prayer, believing, ye shall receive.*

18.   Mark 11:24: *What things soever ye desire when you pray, believe that ye receive them and ye shall have them.*

Signs and Wonders

Jesus taught His disciples *about* the Word of God and also taught them the Word. In all of His teachings, He emphasized that their learning must be merged with faith, and faith with their learning: "*If ye have faith,*" "*believe,*" "*believing.*" In His departure, He commissioned them:

(17) And these signs shall follow them that believe; In my name shall they cast out devils; they shall speak with new tongues; (18) They shall take up serpents; and if they drink any deadly thing, it shall not hurt them; they shall lay hands on the sick, and they shall recover.

(19)So then after the Lord had spoken unto them, he was received up into heaven, and sat on the right hand of God. (20) And they went forth, and preached every where, the Lord working with them, and confirming the word with signs following. Amen. Mark 16:17-20

All that Jesus had taught them, both by precept and by example, He now commissioned them to practice it. Did it work? We have the record that it did. Did they speak with new tongues?

Acts 2:4: *And they were all filled with the Holy Ghost, and began to speak with other tongues, as the Spirit gave them utterance.*

Did they do signs and wonders?

Acts 2:43: *And fear came upon every soul: and many wonders and signs were done by the apostles.*

Their prayer, Acts 4:29-30: *Grant unto thy servants, that with boldness they may speak thy word, (30) By stretching forth thine hand to heal; and that signs and wonders may be done by the name of thy holy child Jesus.*

Acts 14:3: *Long time therefore abode they speaking boldly in the Lord which gave testimony unto the word of his grace, and granted signs and wonders to be done by their hands.*

Many other scriptural citations might be added to these: Acts 15:12; Romans 15:19; 2Corinthians 12:12; Hebrews 1:3; 2:4. However, where faith was not merged with their learning, it did not work:

For unto us was the gospel preached as well as unto them: but the word preached did not profit them, not being mixed with faith in them that heard it. Hebrews 4:2

In addition, in verse 7 of that chapter we are warned: "*Today if ye will hear his voice, harden not your hearts.*"

What Knowledge, Understanding and Wisdom Must Merge With Our Faith?

We must know the love of God:

Though I have the gift of prophecy, and understand all mysteries, and all knowledge, and though I have faith, so that I could remove mountains, and have not charity, [Love], *I am nothing.* 1Corinthians 13:2

(7) Beloved, let us love one another: for love is of God; and every one that loveth is born of God, and knoweth God. (8) He that loveth not knoweth not God; for God is love. (9) In this was manifested the love of God toward us, because that God sent his only begotten Son into the world, that we might live through him. (10) Herein is love, not that we loved God, but that he loved us; and sent his Son to be the propitiation for our sins. (11) Beloved, if God so loved us, we ought to also to love one another. 1John 4:7-11

(2) By this we know that we love the children of God, when we love God and keep his commandments. (3) For this is the love of God, that we keep his commandments and his commandments are not grievous. 1John 5:2-3

God's purpose in creation was motivated by love:

(10) To the intent that now unto the principalities and powers in heavenly places might be known by the church, the manifold wisdom of God, (11)According to the eternal purpose which he purposed in Christ Jesus our Lord:…. (17) That Christ may dwell in your hearts by faith; that ye, being rooted and grounded in love, (18) May be able to comprehend with all saints what is the breadth, and length, and depth, and height; (19) And to know the love of Christ, which passeth knowledge, that ye might be filled with all the fullness of God. Ephesians 3:10-11, 17-19

Until You've Known the Love of God[80]

If you could own all the world and its money

Build castles tall enough to reach the sky above

If you could know everything there is to know about life's game
Still you'd know nothing until you've known God and His love.

Until you've known the loving hand that reaches down to fallen man And lifts him up from out of sin where he has trod Until you've known just how it feels to know that God is really real Then you've known nothing, until you've known the love of God.

---

[80] Words and music by Rusty Goodman, (1933-1990).

If in your lifetime you could meet everybody And you could know every name from here to yon. But if you've not come face to face with Jesus and His saving grace. Then you've known nothing until you've known God and His love.

TA CHARISMATA TA MEIDZONA

Rethinking I Corinthians 12: 31

For Twenty-First Century Pentecostalism

Marvin J. Hudson, D. Min

Much emphasis has been placed in recent decades upon the function of the Holy Spirit within the context of the American church. Without a doubt, the classical Pentecostal denominations of the last century functioned seminally to foster this interest in pneumatology. Added to these influences has been the emergence of the charismatic movement of the mid-twentieth century. The influence of the so-called charismatic renewal movement should not be minimized.

Whatever positive results may have come to the church because of the Pentecostal renewal of the twentieth century, it is a virtual axiom that the Pentecostal and Charismatic expressions of renewal in American Protestantism have been fraught with problems and painful limitations as well. The literature exploring tensions and conflict within congregations of these renewal streams is legion. Many within our ranks could add additional case studies to such a collection.[81] The simple and painful reality is that history bears out that an active interest and participation in the

---

[81] Blumhofer, Edith L., Spittler, Russell P., and Wacker, Grant A. Pentecostal Currents in American Protestantism. p.168ff. In this volume, contributor Nancy L. Eiesland offers a excellent contemporary case study of the tensions that can exist within congregations experiencing the benefits of Pentecostal-Charismatic renewal.

present endowment of the Holy Spirit, does not automatically lead to spiritual maturation.

However, the thrust of this essay is not to explore minutely the contributions or excesses of either stream of tradition over the last century but, rather to reexamine the potential benefit of Paul's understanding of the greater gifts for any and all groups that prize both spiritual unity and the work of the Spirit within their midst. Succinctly stated, the questions posed in this essay are "What is the best definition of the "τα χαρισματα τα μειζονα" ("The greater gifts") to which the Corinthian believers are exhorted? Further, "What is the determinative factor of excellence (τα μειζονα) that is in play in this spiritual category and how is it that the Corinthians (and presumably ourselves) might benefit from their operative presence?

Defining the Context

The concept of gift suggests to most contemporary minds, the idea of something that is presented or given and subsequently taken into possession. Usually, there are no strings attached. Indeed, we tend to look askance at gifts beset by encumbrances. In common parlance, the concept of gift suggests possession and control; i.e. 'one has been gifted with a property and may employ it, as so inclined.'

When the discussion of gift enters the arena of the function of the charismata within the church, the typical presuppositions that we bring to gifts in general may compromise our success. Our fundamental human tendency to selfishness plays well to the concept of gift as an expression of control and self-gratification. Even when the gift experience is benign as in a birthday or anniversary, our foundational psycho-emotional frame of reference is essentially self-gratifying. On the theological front which is often less benign, it has been well documented that the human qualities of intolerance and self-centeredness reflected in theological "absolutism" that have at times characterized twentieth century Pentecostalism have gone hand in hand with expressions of charismata.[82]

There is reason to believe that for the early church, the charisma (το χαρισμα, ατος) moved from being any gracious or favorable gift to the theological technical term to describe the impartation of "That which is freely and graciously given...Of spiritual gifts in a special sense."[83] This view is

---

[82] Grant Wacker, Heaven Below, Early Pentecostals and American Culture. Cambridge, Mass.: Harvard University Press, 2003, p.23-26.
[83] Frederick William Danker, Ed. A Greek-English Lexicon of the New Testament and Other Early Christian Literature, Third Edition. Chicago: University of Chicago Press, 2000, p.1081.

sustained by a survey of the papyri as well.[84] When Paul focuses his attention upon these special gifts in I Corinthians, he does so with certain parameters in mind. First, Paul emphasizes that these gifts are imparted with a condition attached. The condition is that the gifts are set squarely in the context of the Christological confession.[85] The "gifts" are imparted by the Spirit whose primary work is to bear witness to Jesus Christ.[86] Any behavior that does not further this goal is not consistent with the emphasis of the Spirit that imparts the gifts. Paul stresses that there are "varieties of gifts," but the motivation behind each is always the same; working the things of God fully into all.[87] This is nothing less that the goal of achieving completion or perfection within the body of Christ; an image that Paul utilizes elsewhere in his epistles when he speaks of believers coming to the Telos of God. It is to this end that Paul

---

[84] James Hope Moulton, George Milligan, The Vocabulary of the Greek New Testament Illustrated from the Papyri and Other Non-Literary Sources. Grand Rapids: Wm. B. Eerdmans, 1976, p. 685.

[85] I Corinthians 12:1-3.

[86] C.K. Barrett, The First Epistle to the Corinthians. New York: Harper and Row, 1968. p. 283.

[87] I Corinthians 12: 4-6.

Διαιρεσεις δε χαρισματων εισιν, το δε αθτο πνευμα και διαιρεσεις διακονιων εισιν, και ο αυτος κυριος και διαιρεσεις ενεργμαυων εισιν, ο δε αυτος θεος, ο ενεργων τα παντα εν πασιν.

The repetitive emphasis passage of 4-6 builds to the climactic statement that the purpose for the diversity of gifting is that it is God's intention to "work all things in everyone." This is a euphemistic way to speak of the efforts of God through the Holy Spirit to bring the church to the Telos of the God.

continues in verse seven to affirm that these operations (των πνευματικων) are intended to benefit the entire body in the process of growth implied in the prepositional phrase "For the common good" (προς τους συμφερον). This phrase strongly implies a collective advantage or benefit derived from the various individual gifts imparted to believers. To anticipate later discussion, the goal of the "diversities of gifts" is other—oriented as much or more than self-oriented.[88] The import of this selfless emphasis upon the common good is dramatically illustrated in Paul's subsequent discussion of the gifted body of Christ as a physical body either nurturing or rejecting its various parts.[89] The image portrayed within the anatomical analogy is that the diverse gifting of the body may be accompanied by immature responses from some believers towards others. These immature actions actually serve to defeat the fullest expression of reciprocal growth to which the Charisma pointed. From a survey of the context of I Corinthians, it appears that this first century church may have been more than a little susceptible to this type of narcissism. Remember that this was a church with a list of ego tensions such as status divisions, legal conflicts, libertine moral attitudes, abuses of the love feast, to name only a partial list. The

---

[88] Ibid, Danker, "συμφερω", p. 960.
[89] I Corinthians 12: 12-26.

common denominator within all of these appears to have been a narcissistic self-interest that made it difficult for the community to function in ways in keeping with the spirit of Christ.

There is reason to imagine that the sitz-im-leben into which the admonition of chapter twelve is directed is one that employs the same narcissism with relation to the so-called spirituals. Anthony Thiselton argues convincingly that the Corinthians were enticed by the notion that there was a "greater" quality to particular gifts, but incorrectly saw that greatness in terms of "a high social order and/or spiritual status".[90] Thiselton correctly notes that Paul redefines μειζονα in a way that turns normal standards of greatness on their heads. So called "status seeking elitists" are confronted with a new and contrary definition.[91] In this writer's view, this new definition harks back to the flavor of Christ's admonition of who would be called the greatest in the Kingdom. The familiar answer was of course, the one who becomes a servant of all. To extend this line of thought, Paul's use of the body analogy may then appropriately argue that every member of the body needs every other member

---

[90] Anthony C. Thiselton, The First Epistle to the Corinthians, The New International Greek Testament Commentary. Grand Rapids, MI: Wm. B. Eerdmans, 2000, pp. 1024.
[91] ibid. 1025

whether their gifting is spectacular or not, for all have a role of important service.

While the Charismata are appropriately understood as gifts in the sense of an endowment that is freely and graciously given, we may not suppose that they are gifts that are characterized by absolute freedom. It might be helpful if we as Pentecostals could bring ourselves to modify our traditional terminology of 'spiritual gifts' to language that favors terminology reflective of "operations of grace" [92] or "endowments." [93]

This language helps move us away from the comfortable but erroneous notion that the Charismata are gifts to be understood in self-gratifying ways. Paul argues that we do not exercise unlimited freedom. Ideally, the Holy Spirit imparts and inspires the operation of the gifts. Hence, the gifts are expected by Paul to be distinctly non-selfish in their function. The charismata are to enhance the body corporate, not merely individuals. Robert Banks recognizes this corporate perspective when he call to our attention that in Paul's discussion, the setting of the gifts is not the church

---

[92] ibid. Moulton and Milligan, p.685
[93] Hans Conzelmann, First Corinthians, Hermenia. Philadelphia: Fortress Press, 1975, p.208.

(εχχλησια) but the Body (σωμα).[94] This is a Pauline word of choice, emphasizing the other-oriented focus of the charismata. The gifts may well have been exercised within the community gathering, but the focus was always upon the enhancement of the body of Christ. Personal gratification, whether in the form of prestige or ecstasy, takes a secondary role to the function of up building fellow members of the body (οιχοδομη). This is an excellent corrective to many of the historic limitations of twentieth century Pentecostalism and Charismatism. Whatever one might say about the status issues of the dramatic manifestations of the Spirit, there is little doubt that the personal ecstasy involved in the realm of the spiritual (πνευματιχων), was a seductive lure towards spiritual self-absorption. Such a selfish orientation that was at the heart of every issue that the Corinthians faced, is the very antithesis of the Spirit of Christ. All of Paul's remonstrance must be viewed against the image of a commitment to intentionally emulate Christ towards one another.

Defining the Greater Gifts: Principle of Excellence

Paul concludes his intense discussion of the nature and function of spiritual gifts with the admonition, "But earnestly

---

[94] Robert Banks, Paul's Idea of Community: The Early House Churches in Their Historical Setting. Grand Rapids: Eerdmans, 1982, p. 101.

seek the greater gifts." (ζηλουτε δε τα χαρισματα τα μειζονα) [95] What is one to make of this admonition? What, for Paul, would the greater gifts be? Is faith greater than knowledge? Is a miracle greater than administration? By what rubric are believers to make such determinations? An examination of chapter twelve immediately prior to the imperatival in verse 31, around two lines of thought may be helpful.

First, since in the delineation of nine charismata in verses eight through ten, he begins with the "Word of Wisdom" and "Word of Knowledge" and ends with "Tongues" and "Interpretation of Tongues", the "Greater Gifts" could be those first listed. Thus, wisdom and knowledge would be higher on this simple order of priority list. Second, since just prior to the imperative Paul declares that "God has appointed in the church first apostles, second prophets, third teachers, then miracles, then gifts of healing, helps, administrations, various kinds of tongues," the greater gifts could be construed to be apostles and prophets and so-forth. Certainly, it has been suggested that a simple reading of these two lists depict the greater gifts based on their order.[96] An obvious difficulty with this idea is that the latter

---

[95] ζηλουτε may be either indicative or imperative. Most translations understand the logic of the imperative.

[96] Gordon D. Fee, The First Epistle to the Corinthians, The New International Commentary on the New Testament. Grand Rapids: Wm B. Eerdmans Publishling Company, 1987, p.623.

list does not stand on its own. One must factor the earlier list of charismata. When one includes the second list, internal inconsistencies are apparent.

vv 8-10	v 28
Wisdom	Apostles
Knowledge	Prophets
Faith	Teachers
Healing	Miracles
Prophecy	Helps
Spiritual Discernment	Administration
Tongues	Tongues
Interpretations	

Note that there are charismata present in both lists that do not carry over to the other list. Additionally, the simple order is not consistent as well. For example, Prophecy is, if the simple ranking concept were valid, number six in vv. 8-10, but number two in v. 28. Other characteristics appear to be 'all over the place' in terms of the twin lists. One element of consistency is related to the gift of tongues. In both lists, it is essentially last. Some writers have suggested that Paul's reason for listing tongues virtually last in both lists lay in this ranking concept. Typically, they suggest that Paul understood this gift to be either problematic with the Corinthians or essentially non-beneficial. To an extent, this may be valid, but not from the perspective of anti-Pentecostal bias that has been present in some twentieth century scholarship.

It is a compelling idea that Corinth had a problem with correct perspective about how to live in the community of Christ. They did appear to be attracted to elements of both temporal life and faith that were ego gratifying. Because of the highly ecstatic nature of tongues as manifested in the New Testament,[97] it is tempting to think that Paul may have listed it last because it could be corrupted to the passions of the carnal self. Nor does the placement of tongues at the end of the twin lists constitute a compelling argument that a simple ranking of the lists is sufficient to determine the identity of the greater gifts. To return to the example of

---

[97] Consider that the Acts 2 account of the outpouring of the Holy Spirit portrays an event that portrays an event ecstatic in nature. Further, other stories of similar events suggest something that was powerful and attractive, e.g. Simon Magus in Acts 8, who witnesses something that is so dramatic that he is willing to purchase the ability.

prophecy, we have seen that in the first list, Paul places it sixth, and in the second list, it ranks second. However, when Paul takes up the discussion of this gift of prophecy in chapter fourteen, it jumps to a pre-eminent status. Such gyrations make it difficult to know with certainty how important prophecy is if we employ a simple ranking order.

What is our alternative then? How does Paul define the greater gifts? The definition of the Meizona lies not with order in and of itself, but in another issue entirely. Wisdom, knowledge, apostleship, or prophetic offices are not to be construed as the greater gifts simply because they are higher on the list. Rather the essence of τα χαρισματα τα μειζονα is discovered in the underlying theology of Paul's letter. Early in the paper, it was noted that the function of the Spirit was to point to Christ. That pointing action within the Pauline house church was two-fold. First and arbitrarily for our discussion, the Spirit functioned within the community in an equipping or nurturing manner. The goal was to foster spiritual growth and maturation on the part of individual members of the community. Second, this growth was to find its logical expression in the area of ministry, inclusive of evangelism. The result was a cyclical organic movement of nurture, growth, and outreach. This is consistent with other passages that discuss spiritual growth within the community as an interrelated process.[98]

For Paul's house church theology, the Charismata (gifts) are imparted for the primary purpose of facilitating spiritual growth within the community. This does not rule out the possible secondary emphasis of certain gifts having direct implications for ministry beyond the community, but that Paul's emphasis within the Corinthian correspondence is upon internal actions.[99] In this specific setting, Paul stresses that the gifts of the Spirit are tools of corporate edification that are to be employed to build up others within the body of Christ. By design, it is through this agency that God's growth is imparted. Thus, the Ta Meizona Ta Charismata are defined and ranked with respect to the degree to which they benefit others more than ourselves. Because Paul emphasizes that the loftiest goal one can attain to is the emulation of the Spirit of Christ, behaviors such as the Corinthians were guilty of are unthinkable within the community. All such practices such as schisms, lawsuits, immorality, or selfish employment of the Charismata, fail the test of selflessness that is the essence of Christ. The injunction to desire the

---

[98] E.g. Colossians 2:19, 15. Ephesians 4: 11-16.

[99] Certain spirituals or gifts such as proclamation or miracles and perhaps others could potentially function as semeia. As such, they could offer validation to the witness of the evangelical church. Cf. I Corinthians 2: 1-5.

greater gifts is an injunction to be possessed of such gifts as will empower servant ministry. The Τα Μειζονα Τα Χαρισματα is not a list, but a question, "What gifts most directly benefit others in their journey towards perfection."

The Corinthian Corrective

The corrective of I Corinthians 12: 31 in its extended context was urgently needed within the Corinthian church. The total portrait we receive from this letter is of a community in turmoil and conflict. While they apparently prized the Gospel they had received and esteemed the spirituals that attended it, they did so within the context of a very flawed value system. In colloquial terms, they were attempting to live a new community life from an old community context. Defeat was the result. As the self was asserted, the principle of servant hood and graceful reciprocity depicted in the body analogy was abandoned. Self-gratification and dysfunctional behavior became normative within at least significant segments of the community.

Their lesson is ours as well. As has been noted, the twentieth century Pentecostal movement in all of its forms has also both prized the Gospel and the spirituals as well. However, we have experienced our own discipleship battles.

We find it easy to think of ourselves before others—to emphasize the personal and existentially gratifying over those gifts that propel us into service. It is not by coincidence that Paul punctuates his discussion of spiritual gifts with chapter thirteen that in all probability functions as an excursus on the driving force behind both the definition of the τα μειζονα τα χαρισματα, and the motivation to eagerly seek them. Love calls us into reciprocal nurture through the power of the Holy Spirit.

[1] Blumhofer, Edith L., Spittler, Russell P., and Wacker, Grant A. Pentecostal Currents in American Protestantism. p.168ff. In this volume, contributor Nancy L. Eiesland offers a excellent contemporary case study of the tensions that can exist within congregations experiencing the benefits of Pentecostal-Charismatic renewal.

[1] Grant Wacker, Heaven Below, Early Pentecostals and American Culture. Cambridge, Mass.: Harvard University Press, 2003, p.23-26.

[1] Frederick William Danker, Ed. A Greek-English Lexicon of the New Testament and Other Early Christian Literature, Third Edition. Chicago: University of Chicago Press, 2000, p.1081.

[1] James Hope Moulton, George Milligan, The Vocabulary of the Greek New Testament Illustrated from the Papyri and Other Non-Literary Sources. Grand Rapids: Wm. B. Eerdmans, 1976, p. 685.

[1] I Corinthians 12:1-3.

[1] C.K. Barrett, The First Epistle to the Corinthians. New York: Harper and Row, 1968. p. 283.

[1] I Corinthians 12: 4-6.

Διαιρεσεις δε χαρισματων εισιν, το δε αθτο πνευμα και διαιρεσεις διακονιων εισιν, και ο αυτος κυριος και διαιρεσεις ενεργμαυων εισιν, ο δε αυτος θεος, ο ενεργων τα παντα εν πασιν.

The repetitive emphasis passage of 4-6 builds to the climactic statement that the purpose for the diversity of gifting is that it is God's intention to "work all things in everyone." This is a euphemistic way to speak of the efforts of God through the Holy Spirit to bring the church to the Telos of the God.

[1] Ibid, Danker, "συμφερω", p. 960.

[1] I Corinthians 12: 12-26.

[1] Anthony C. Thiselton, The First Epistle to the Corinthians, The New International Greek Testament Commentary. Grand Rapids, MI: Wm. B. Eerdmans, 2000, pp. 1024.

[1] ibid. 1025

[1] ibid. Moulton and Milligan, p.685

[1] Hans Conzelmann, First Corinthians, Hermenia. Philadelphia: Fortress Press, 1975, p.208.

[1] Robert Banks, Paul's Idea of Community: The Early House Churches in Their Historical Setting. Grand Rapids: Eerdmans, 1982, p. 101.

[1] ζηλουτε may be either indicative or imperative. Most translations understand the logic of the imperative.

[1] Gordon D. Fee, The First Epistle to the Corinthians, The New International Commentary on the New Testament. Grand Rapids: Wm B. Eerdmans Publishling Company, 1987, p.623.

[1] Consider that the Acts 2 account of the outpouring of the Holy Spirit portrays an event that portrays an event ecstatic in nature. Further, other

stories of similar events suggest something that was powerful and attractive, e.g. Simon Magus in Acts 8, who witnesses something that is so dramatic that he is willing to purchase the ability.

[1] E.g. Colossians 2:19, 15. Ephesians 4: 11-16.

[1] Certain spirituals or gifts such as proclamation or miracles and perhaps others could potentially function as semeia. As such, they could offer validation to the witness of the evangelical church. Cf. I Corinthians 2: 1-5.

Analysis of Pentecostal Mission Strategy

by

Rev. Kenneth L. Young

The dynamic growth of Christianity during the 19th century prompted eminent church historian, Kenneth Scott Latourette, to designate it as "the great century" in his voluminous composition. "Never before had Christianity, or any religion, been introduced to so many different peoples and cultures. Never before in a period of equal length had Christianity or any other religion penetrated for the first time as large an area as it had in the nineteenth century. Never before had so many hundreds of thousands contributed voluntarily of their means to assist the spread of Christianity or any other religion."[1] Consequently, Christianity experienced its greatest advance to date during this period. However, with the introduction of a new "Pentecost" in 1901 and because of the World Missionary Conference of 1910 in Edinburgh, Scotland, the 20th century would prove to be a "greater century" of growth than its immediate predecessor. While the nineteenth century exhibited a 172 percent rate of growth in Christianity, the twentieth century featured an astounding growth rate of 261 percent.[2]

The advent of Pentecostalism at the turn of the century (most readily revealed in and through the Azusa Street revival), and the global impact of the World Missionary Conference offered Christianity both eschatological and ecumenical motivations for mission strategy. The belief in the imminent return of Jesus Christ stimulated the eschatological aspect, whereas entreaty for theological education, missionary preparation, ecclesiastical cooperation, and joint communication marked the ecumenical component.

During the early period, most Pentecostals embraced the former method; very few of them incorporated the latter. This paper analyzes early Pentecostal mission strategy, assessing the effect of early eschatological expectations on that strategy and comparing it with present day, ecumenical methods and strategy; the work concentrates on the previous eschatological emphasis of early Pentecostals and the contemporary methods and tactics of the World Missions Ministries (WMM) of the International Pentecostal Holiness Church (IPHC).

What existed in Pentecostalism that caused its exponential growth and worldwide acceptance? What motivated the early Pentecostal missionaries? This author posits that the early Pentecostals emphasized hope in an era of seemingly hopelessness; this eschatological dimension of Pentecostalism motivated their missionary enterprise. The impetus may have been the experience and doctrine of the "Baptism in the Holy Spirit," but the motivation was the

"Second Coming of Christ." Their reasoning was more eschatological than pneumatological. Commenting on the personal account of English pastor and missionary to Norway, Thomas B. Barratt, Pentecostal church historian, Vinson Synan argues, "His testimony reveals the overriding ethos of Pentecostalism: the urgency to evangelize the world ahead of the imminent return of Jesus Christ."[3] Expectation, excitement, and assurance characterized these pioneers.

The Pentecostal experience presaged the "last days." The goal was world evangelism and the motivation, the return of Christ. For example, The Thirteenth Article of Faith of the IPHC states, "We believe in the imminent, personal, premillennial second coming of our Lord Jesus Christ and love and wait for His appearing."[4] One of the elemental words in this credence of early Pentecostalism was "imminent." Imminence means "the quality or condition of being about to occur."[5] The word connotes the future but accentuates immediacy and impendency.

Since most Pentecostals believed that the outpouring of the Holy Spirit indicated the end times and, consequently, the immediacy of the return of the Lord, their objectives included world evangelism. Indeed, the Fourteenth Article of Faith of the IPHC says, "We believe it is the responsibility of every believer to dedicate his life to carrying out the work of the Great Commission."[6] This last article ensues logically the previous one regarding the impending return of Christ; likewise, it follows purposefully. "This has not always been clearly enunciated, as Pentecostal missionaries got on with the job in a hurry, believing that the time was short and that reflection about the task was not as important as action in evangelism."[7]

Indubitably, Pentecostals deemed that empowerment by the Holy Sprit impelled them to world missions because the coming of the Lord was imminent. The doctrinal emphasis of early Pentecostal teacher and preacher, Charles Fox Parham, stimulated this initiative.

Many of the early Pentecostals based their mission strategy on the doctrine that Charles Parham propagated. "He has claimed that through their baptism in the Spirit, those who spoke in tongues were being specially equipped to carry out God's end time global missionary mandate."[8] Again, the impulse was eschatological, not pneumatological. Parham believed correctly that the tongues, which people articulated, were foreign languages; however, he misinterpreted, in the opinion of this writer, the implications of this credence. Parham taught that whatever tongue (foreign language) a person verbalized when she or he received the baptism in the Holy Spirit would direct the person to the country where and the people whom she or he should proclaim the Gospel. Synan elucidates, "Parham immediately began teaching that Christian missionaries would have no further need of language training. They needed only to receive the baptism with the Holy Spirit and they would be miraculously empowered to speak whatever language was necessary. This was a teaching Parham would steadfastly maintain throughout the rest of his life, despite ever mounting evidence that this was not substantiated by later events."[9] The tenacious eschatological impulse of Parham eclipsed any ecumenical motivation that the World Missionary Conference conveyed. Consequently, the dogma of Parham influenced numerous faithful and rightly galvanized Pentecostals.

The Azusa Street Mission represents a large group of Pentecostals who adhered to the notion of Parham. Cecil M. Roebeck, Jr. accentuates this group in his history of the Azusa Street revival; he describes the procedure that the leadership used to verify and support missionaries.

Essentially, when someone spoke in a tongue, the mission followed a simple four-step program. First, they attempted to identify the language. Second, if they felt they had identified it, they sought to establish whether the speaker believed he or she had a received, a missionary "call." Third, if the tongues-speaker claimed to have such a call, the mission staff tried to discern whether the call was genuine and whether the person was ready and willing to go. Finally, if the person testified to a readiness to go, and the mission discerned the necessary gifts and call, then they gave the candidate the money to reach the foreign field, and he or she left town within days, if not hours.[10]

The Azusa Street Mission dispatched many missionaries from its ranks in this manner. Indeed, the mission staff practiced a methodology, albeit minimal, for sanctioning a candidate, but their eschatological zeal caused them to impede the other training methods suggested by the World Missionary Conference (theological education, missionary preparation, ecclesiastical cooperation, and joint communication). This impediment resulted in labeling these devotees as "missionaries of the one way ticket." Tragically, some died on the mission field due to their lack of strategic planning; others, upon arrival to their designated country or people group, discovered that their "missionary tongue" was not the language of this country or its people!

Eschatology proved itself motivationally, but it also refuted itself methodologically. The numbers of dispatched

Pentecostal missionaries and the tragic outcomes of many disclose this dichotomy. "In numerous cases, their overall impact proved short-lived and disappointing. Disillusionment crept in as harsh realities deified their best efforts."[11] Roebeck concurs with this analysis from Synan: "Most of these folks lasted on the foreign field between six months and a year, especially when their initial expectations were disappointed."[12] However, one should not judge the idealism; rather, evaluate the ignorance. Motive, based on eschatological fervor, proved itself veritable, but method, established on this same ardor, exposed its own vulnerability.

These faithful missionaries founded their idealism upon their eschatological hope of the *Parousia*. Some died for this hope; others persevered by learning to adapt through flexibility, not in their eschatological theology but in their methodological strategy. Synan identifies the importunate missionaries as the ones who "survived by learning the language, adjusting to different cultural contexts, and adapting to the challenges that confronted them."[13] These pioneers embraced their idealistic eschatology awhile assimilating a realistic methodology.

For example, Thomas Junk discovered that he had arrived in northern China without the ability to speak any Chinese dialect. Instead of returning to America in defeat, he decided to acclimate to his mission field. "He took that discovery in stride and began to study the language...eating Chinese food, learning the Chinese language, and going to areas that other missionaries had rejected because of the primitive conditions there."[14] His missiological fervor, fueled by his eschatological expectation yet now informed by his methodological realism, inspired Junk to remain and serve in the country where he believed God had directed him.

Other voices who entreated early Pentecostal missions to consider and require proper training include Alexander A. Boddy, an Anglican Priest who received his "baptism in the Holy Spirit," John G. Lake, an Azusa Street Missionary to South Africa, and Antoinette Moomau, another Azusa Street missionary serving in Shang-hai. Boddy "helped the early burgeoning global Apostolic Faith movement by fostering comprehensive theological discussions."[15] Lake insisted on local and long-term financial support as well as cross-cultural training before sending missionaries to foreign fields. Moomau "weighed in on the subject of missionary preparation with two equally pointed concerns of her own.

One of these related to the level of maturity necessary for a missionary to accomplish anything of value."[16] She challenged the notion that one needs only the "baptism in the Holy Spirit" in order to minister effectively on foreign fields. She also identified the requisite for missionaries to settle among the people to whom they were ministering.

Moomau "protested that 'many of these "touring missionaries" do not accomplish much. If they have a real message, it is felt and known, but some drift about, and nothing is accomplished'."[17] These pioneer missionaries and educators represent early voices who implored missionary preparation along with eschatological motive among early Pentecostals. Entreaties similar to these and genuine concern for global evangelization initiated international and ecumenical attention. The World Missionary Conference (WMC) of 1910 was the result of this facilitation.

While the advent of Pentecostalism represented effectively the eschatological motivation of mission strategy in the twentieth century, the WMC of 1910, emphasizing theological education, missionary preparation, ecclesiastical cooperation, and joint communication, denoted substantially the ecumenical motivation. Mainline churches recognized the necessity and practicality of pertinent training. Eventually, Pentecostal mission strategy modified its approach to resemble these ecclesiastical bodies. Ironically, the very tenet of faith, which induced the evangelistic fervency of Pentecostalism, influenced changes in its mission strategy. "As the Lord delayed His coming, Pentecostals realized that building Christ's church required more than signs and wonders. As a result, their methods came to closely resemble those of other evangelical missionaries, but with a unique emphasis on the Spirit's activities."[18]

Pentecostals adopted many of the stratagems of other mission agencies. For example, the IPHC initiated two educational ventures: Franklin Springs Institute (now Emmanuel College) in the southeast and Southwestern Pentecostal Holiness College (now Southwestern Christian University) in the southwest. The IPHC situated these in the two largest regions of its constituency. Additionally, the IPHC required missionaries to raise and sustain their support; this prerequisite offered the missionaries some assurance after they arrived on their fields of service. Moreover, the IPHC interviewed and trained, though minimally, candidates for missionary service. The training included cross cultural communication, indigenization, and even languages. The work of William H. Turner, IPHC missionary to China during the turbulent years of the 1930's and 1940's, illustrates this new strategy. Turner recounts, "I did propose in my heart to try to produce some books on Pentecostal subjects as the Lord enabled me to do so.... I wrote a small tract, the subject of which was: 'Jesus Christ,' and handed it over to Mr. Lee Hung Pien to translate. This was published, first in Cantonese and later in Kwok Yue or Mandarin. It has served a real need and run through many additions and into hundreds of thousands of copies."[19]

Turner authored and translated many more texts and became the first Director of Missions in the IPHC (1961-1965). Pentecostals were realizing that the "sign of tongues" demonstrated more of the power to accomplish ministry than it pointed to specific fields in which to minister. Finally, Pentecostals recognized and appreciated ecumenical endeavors. "In the late 1960s affiliations were initiated with sister Pentecostal bodies abroad. The first international affiliation was with the Pentecostal Methodist Church of Chili in 1967, followed by a similar agreement with the Wesleyan Methodist Church of Brazil in 1983."[20] Presently, the IPHC continues to collaborate with analogous believers worldwide.

The delay of the Parousia forced Pentecostals generally and the IPHC particularly to reevaluate their strategy. However, their assurance of the imminent return of Christ – no matter how long the Father delays this – and their assessment of the outpouring of the Holy Spirit still impel their missionary enterprise. The outpouring of the Holy Spirit remains the impetus for sharing the Gospel; the Parousia, informed by ecumenicism, the motivation. The web page of the WMM of the IPHC typifies current Pentecostal missionary methods and strategies. It purports both eschatological and ecumenical motives for advancing the Gospel. It reads as follows:

The primary purpose of the World Missions Ministries of the International Pentecostal Holiness Church is to fulfill the Great Commission of our Lord Jesus Christ. This includes:

- The proclamation of the gospel and the conversion of the lost to Jesus Christ.

- The planting of indigenous churches.

- The equipping of spiritual leaders of these churches.

- The incorporation of these indigenous churches into one worldwide fellowship.

- the expansion of the Pentecostal revival throughout the body of Christ.[21]

The first part of the mission statement focuses on the single purpose of the WMM: to obey the Great Commission of Christ. The second part accentuates the methods the IPHC intends to use in order to accomplish this task. The first and fifth strategies emphasize the eschatological component, the second, third, and fourth, the ecumenical. These elements demonstrate that the IPHC has learned some arduous lessons from history. The challenge is for Pentecostals to retain their eschatological expectations while embracing other, inveterate ecumenical methods.

How, then, can Pentecostals contribute positively to the Church universal in exceeding the phenomenal growth of the previous two centuries? Moreover, how do Pentecostals maintain their eschatological influence as well as enhance their ecumenical progress? This author elucidates three essential facets of Pentecostal missions for the twenty-first century. These facets incorporate biblical, theological, and sociological distinctives. Pentecostal missions in the twenty-first century require biblical concentricity, theological accuracy, and sociological relevancy.

Pentecostal missions require primarily a biblical basis. The WMM statement declares its commitment to the command of Jesus Christ to "make disciples of all the nations, baptizing them into the name of the Father and the Son and the Holy Spirit, teaching them to adhere to all which I commanded you...."[22] This commitment necessitates that the IPHC not only obey the command of Christ but also conform to his missionary enterprise. Noel Brooks highlights this missional venture of Christ: "It is not enough for us to go out in a 'deliverance' ministry. It is not enough for us to go out with an eschatological teaching. We must have as a fundamental, as a foundation, as a dynamic aspect, of the message which we proclaim, the facts of the Gospel, the death and resurrection of Jesus Christ."[23] Even a Pentecostal methodology should emphasize primarily the foundation of the gospel – the crucifixion and resurrection of Jesus Christ. We evangelize principally for Christ to build his Church, not our own institution. Brooks contends, "Fundamentally, we are not sent to the mission field to build a denominational church."[24] Pentecostals must recognize that Christ is working in and through them to build his Church, not their organization. Biblical concentricity proceeds systematically and produces naturally theological accuracy. When Pentecostals acknowledge and sanction this primacy, then they may emphasize the biblical theology of the Holy Spirit because this is their unique contribution to the Church.

Pentecostals offer the Church and, consequently, the world an inimitable theological expediency. The empowerment of the Holy Spirit endows the Church with the impetus to evangelize and educate all peoples. This empowerment and endowment is the unique, theological gift that Pentecostalism offers the Church. Synan recognizes accurately that "Pentecostalism in its various forms has changed the landscape of Christianity and introduced an authentic Trinitarian praxis of mission."[25]

The God of the Bible is a missional god: the Father sends the Son and the Son sends the Spirit and the Spirit sends us. The Spirit endows the Church with the *charisms* to reconcile the world to God. The onus rests upon Pentecostal theologians to describe accurately and its theological institutions to teach appropriately this religious phenomenon. Theological veracity requires Pentecostals to investigate the whole of Scripture, not simply to consider a few chapters and verses. Biblical concentricity informs theological accuracy. This contingency guides the Church to sociological relevancy.

The present exponential growth and global acceptance of Pentecostalism has caused it to disregard its sociological past. Having been once ignored and neglected, Pentecostals have now forgotten the poor, the marginalized, the outcasts, and the oppressed. In their desire to escape a poverty mentality, many Pentecostals have disregarded those who are still ensnared in similar circumstances. Anderson recognizes this negligence; he analyzes accordingly: "Unfortunately, the emphasis on self-propagation through evangelism and church growth has sometimes resulted in Pentecostals being somewhat inward looking and seemingly unconcerned or oblivious to the serious issues of the socio-political contexts."[26] While Pentecostals minister to immediate needs of indigenous people groups, they tend to overlook the macrocosm that caused the local dilemmas. Indeed, the second, third, and fourth methods in the WMM mission statement declare its intentional aspiration of planting, training, and incorporating indigenous peoples. Yet, the IPHC must address also the local and global comprehensive affairs that threaten these nationals.

The WMM of the IPHC should expand its modern strategy to include macroeconomic and socio-political subject matter while continuing to advance indigenous objectives. Anderson and this author concede that Pentecostals are beginning to recognize the social implications of the gospel, [27] but much work remains unfinished in this realm.

One vital area which Christian denominations generally and the IPHC particularly disregard is the requisite of Bible translation. This evaluator opines that the IPHC and its WMM must ruminate intentionally on Bible translation as a mission strategy. Proper indigenization requires a Bible in the language of the people. As Mark Devine stipulates, "The sooner a ministry becomes indigenous to its culture the sooner it could spread like wildfire."[28] What better way to influence a culture than to offer it a Bible in its own language! Resultantly, the WMM could realize all five, methodological principles. This author proposes and advocates that the WMM of the IPHC investigate this rudimentary factor of indigenization. The WMM could become the vanguard of Pentecostalism in this indispensable endeavor, and its impact could make the twenty-first century the "greatest" in Christianity.

Notes

1. Quoted in Winthrop S. Hudson, *Religion in America*, second edition (New York: Charles Scribner's Sons, 1973), 157.

2. David B. Barrett and Todd M. Johnson, "Status of Global Mission, Presence, and Activities, AD 1800-2025," *International Bulletin of Missionary Research*, vol. 32, No. 1, January, 2008, http://www.gordonconwell.edu/ockenga/globalchristianity/resources.php (accessed March 19, 2008).

3. J.A. Synan, *Old Time Power: A History of the Pentecostal Holiness Church* (Franklin Springs, GA: LifeSprings, 1998), 71.

4. International Pentecostal Holiness Church, "Articles of Faith," *The 2005 Manual of the International Pentecostal Holiness Church*, http://arc.iphc.org/theology/artfaith.html (accessed June 25, 2008).

5. *American Heritage College Dictionary, The* (4th edition), s.v. "imminence."

6. IPHC, "Articles of Faith," (accessed June 25, 2008).

7. Allan H. Anderson, "Towards a Pentecostal Missiology," ArtsWeb, University of Birmingham, 1998, http://artsweb.bham.ac.uk.htm (accessed June 25, 2008).

8. Cecil M. Roebeck, Jr., *The Azusa Street Mission & Revival: The Birth of the Global Pentecostal Movement* (Nashville, TN: Thomas Nelson, Inc., 2006), 236.

9. Synan, *Old Time Power*, 44.

10. Roebeck, *Azusa Street Mission*, 239.

11. J.A. Synan, *The Century of the Holy Spirit: 100 Years of Pentecostal and Charismatic Renewal* (Nashville, TN: Thomas Nelson Publishers, 2001), 81.

12. Roebeck, *Azusa Street Mission*, 243.

13. Synan, *The Century of the Holy Spirit*, 81.

14. Roebeck, *Azusa Street Mission*, 259.

15. Ibid., 247.

16. Ibid., 248.

17. Ibid., 250.

18. Synan, *The Century of the Holy Spirit*, 94.

19. William H. Turner, *Building for God in War, Blood and Death* (Athens, GA: The McGregor Company, 1947), 166.

20. International Pentecostal Holiness Church, "History: Organizational Developments," May 19, 1996, http://www.iphc.org/docs/hisdev.html (accessed September 17, 2008).

21. International Pentecostal Holiness Church, "World Missions Ministries," http://wmm.iphc.org/structur.html (accessed September 7, 2009).

22. Unless indicated otherwise, all New Testament passages are the translation of this author from Eberhard Nestle and Kurt Aland, ed., *Novum Testamentum Graece*, 27th ed. (Stuttgart: Deutsche Bibelgesellschaft, 1993), 87.

23. Noel Brooks, *The Biblical Basis for Missions* (Franklin Springs, GA: Advocate Press, 1976), 49.

24. Ibid., 61.

25. Synan, *The Century of the Holy Spirit*, 94.

26. Anderson, "Towards a Pentecostal Missiology," 3.

27. Ibid., 3.

28. Mark Devine, "The Emerging Church: One Movement – Two Streams," in *Evangelicals Engaging Emergent: A Discussion of the Emergent Church Movement*, ed. William D. Henard and Adam W. Greenway (Nashville, TN: B & H Publishing Group, 2009), 13-14.

Bibliography

Anderson, Alan H. "Towards a Pentecostal Missiology," ArtsWeb, University of Birmingham, 1998. http://www.artsweb.bham.ac.uk.htm (accessed June 25, 2008).

Barrett, David B. and Todd Johnson. "Status of Global Mission, Presence, and Activities, AD 1800-2025." *International Bulletin of Missionary Research*, vol. 32, No. 1. January, 2008.

Brooks, Noel. *The Biblical Basis for Missions*. Franklin Springs, GA: Advocate Press, 1976.

Devine, Mark. "The Emerging Church: One Movement – Two Streams." In *Evangelicals Engaging Emergents: A Discussion of the Emergent Church Movement*, edited by William D. Henard and Adam W. Greenway, 4-46. Nashville, TN: B & H Publishing Group, 2009.

Hudson, Winthrop S. *Religion in America*, 2nd ed. New York: Charles Scribner's Sons, 1973.

International Pentecostal Holiness Church. "Article Thirteen," *Articles of Faith*, http://arc.iphc.org/theology/artfaith.html (accessed September 7, 2009).

International Pentecostal Holiness Church. "Article Fourteen," *Articles of Faith*, http://arc.iphc.org/theology/artfaith.html (accessed September 7, 2009).

International Pentecostal Holiness Church, "History: Organizational Developments," May 19, 1996. http://www.iphc.org/docs/hisdev.html (accessed September 17, 2008).

International Pentecostal Holiness Church, "World Missions Ministries," http://wmm.iphc.org/structur.html (accessed September 7, 2009).

Jenkins, Philip. *The Next Christendom: The Coming of Global Christianity.* New York: Oxford University Press, 2002.

Nestle, Eberhard and Kurt Aland, ed. *Novum Testamentum Graece*, 27th ed. Stuttgart: Deutsche Bibelgesellschaft, 1993.

Roebeck, Cecil M., Jr. *The Azusa Street Mission & Revival: The Birth of the Global Pentecostal Movement.* Nashville, TN: Thomas Nelson, Inc., 2006.

Synan, Vinson. *The Century of the Holy Spirit: 100 Years of Pentecostal and Charismatic Renewal.* Nashville, TN: Thomas Nelson Publishers, 2001.

Synan, Vinson. *The Old Time Power: A History of the Pentecostal Church.* Franklin Springs, GA: LifeSprings, 1999.

Prophetic Women:

Corinth, Carthage and California - a Continuum of Presence

By

Marilyn A. Hudson

Modern Pentecostalism is generally understood to be firmly rooted in a largely egalitarian holiness movement that recognized the leadership of women such as Catherine Booth, Phoebe Palmer and many others.[100] Modern Pentecostalism (which here will include the traditional Pentecostals, Charismatic, and more recent forms) can be conflicted as it wrestles with its heritage, faith, and cultural influences.

Some affirm the reality of modern prophetic women while others continue to limit woman's participation in spiritual or de facto leadership.[101] The results are often ambiguous and inconsistent in the face of women who identify themselves as 'prophetic.' This ongoing tension is to the general detriment of both genders as it often merely compounds one ambiguous subject with another.

Examining some notable prophetic women of the Bible and history helps clarify the discussion while providing valuable insight. Revealed is then an internal consistency in how women have functioned as true prophets and leaders under the direction and blessing of the Holy Spirit

---

[100] Synan, Vinson, ed. *The Century of the Holy Spirit: 100 years of Pentecostal and Charismatic renewal*. Nashville, Tennessee: Nelson, 2001, pg. 231f.

[101] Keller, Rosemary Skinner. *Encyclopedia of Women & Religion in North America*. Indiana University, 2006, pg. 493.

throughout Biblical and religious history. [102] Yet, it can be said, despite decades of claimed inclusion, social change, and the growth of global Pentecostalism, that the story of women as "prophets" is still an under explored aspect within both Biblical studies and Pentecostal historicity.

Women Prophets in the Bible

In Biblical studies, the prophet is a messenger between God and humanity who engages in some form of proclamation. [103] As a visionary, seer, messenger, covenant mediator, teacher, speaker, spiritual motivator, singer, or in some manner especially gifted (charismata), the prophet was given information to be conveyed to the people. [104] The Spirit of God descended, anointed, guided, impressed, or revealed in some means messages used to achieve specific goals. Sharing messages in some form of proclamation, such as speech or song, they blessed the people and shared the word of God. It is also clear that there were more prophets operating in diverse settings than is often expressed in

---

[102] Madigan, Kevin and Carolyn Osiek, ed. *Ordination of Women in the Early Church: A Documentary History.* John Hopkins University, 2005.

[103] *Dictionary of Biblical Imagery.* IVO, 1998, pg. 668-674.

[104] Yocum, Bruce. *Prophecy exercising the prophetic gifts of the spirit in the church today.* Word of Life, 1976.

popular writings.[105] The prophets warned of the consequences of abandoning the faith, of forgetting to whom they belonged as people of God, and foretold events.[106] The fundamental test of a prophet, moreover, was always that their words proved true.[107]

Sources often reveal frequent attempts to distance women from such leader roles and in many reference works they are totally absent. Arguments have sought to establish artificial linguistic barriers between the terms "prophet" and a "prophetess." Further research, however, indicates no major difference exists between the two terms. Modern society employs the terms "actor" and "actress" merely to label gender for persons in the same field.[108] In several translations the terms "prophet" and "prophetess", however, were used to both identify gender and assign cultural value based solely on the gender. Recent scholarship challenges such false constructions based on gender. Some have even

---

[105] Wilson, Robert R. *Prophecy and society in Ancient Israel*. Fortress, 1952, pg. 223.

[106] Metzger, Bruce, ed. *The Oxford Companion to the Bible*. New York: Oxford University Press, 1993, pg. 622.

[107107] Several verses of the Bible speak directly to this testing: Deut. 18.22, Jer., 28,9, and Mt. 7.20.

[108108] Newsom, Carole, ed. Women's Bible Commentary. Pg. 477.

identified prophetic guilds of women prophets who may have served in warrior, funerary, or scribal capacities.[109] Much more research in ancient Hebrew and archaeology will need to verify those suggestions. The major female prophets as revealed in the Bible, however, already provide very adequate portrayals of the broad function and role of such women. What is required are eyes willing to see what the stories reveal.

Miriam

In Exodus 15:20-21 the people of Israel, freed from the shackles of servitude and slavery, offered praises to God for having been brought out of Egypt. Miriam "the prophetess" took a musical instrument similar to a tambourine and led the women in responsive singing and celebratory dances urging all to "Sing you to the Lord..." Bruggeman suggests one of the primary functions of some prophets was the role of communal or spiritual energizer.[110] In essence, a type of worship leader who served to bring the

---

[109] Gadney, Wilda. *Daughters of Miriam: Women prophets in ancient Israel*. Fortress, 2008.

[110] Brueggemann, Walter. *The Prophetic Imagination*. 2nd ed. Fortress, 2001, pg.16.

people to God and proclaimed His will. Miriam clearly was a dynamic motivating spiritual leader.

Her one failure, along with her brother Aaron, was to question God's choice of Moses. She was struck with leprosy as punishment. The people held her in such regard, however, they waited on her healing before moving forward. Nowhere is there any indication her correction was a comment or judgment on her role as a spiritual leader. Nowhere is there a indictment of her as a leader in general.

Indeed, as an indicator of her status in Jewish history it must be noted that Micah 6:4 recognizes here as one of the prophets **sent by God**. These all indicate that she was a true prophet, a leader, and a woman of God.

Deborah

Deborah was a prophet and judge in the Ephraim hill country of ancient Israel, between Ramah and Bethel. Israel had been living in a tense time the previous twenty years under the oppression of a Canaanite named Sisera. Judges 4:3 says the people "cried unto the Lord."

Deborah is identified as de facto judge and prophet. Note several things about this Judges story convey her role and status in ancient Israel. Deborah was accessible in a public place (similar to the way later elders would sit at the city gates). She acted with authority. The prophet sent for Barack. He was some distance away in the northern reaches of Israel in Nephtali, but hurried to respond and come to where she sat in council. People recognized her as a spiritual and military leader in her role as prophet-judge. Her commander immediately summoned soldiers from other regions. All factors combined indicate Deborah was a major judge perhaps *because* of her multiple office as spiritual and government leader.

A capable woman of many talents able to lead, plan, supervise, direct, and adjure, Deborah was also the spiritual link between God and the people. Like the future king David, there was a touch of the creative as well. The haunting and powerful victory poem "Song of Deborah", with its evocative and very feminine allusions,[111] is thought to be one of the earliest writings of ancient Israel.

---

[111] Holy Bible. KJV. Judges 5.28 is an example, "The mother of Sisera looked through the window, and cried out through the lattice, 'why is his chariot so long in coming…'" reveals a clear understanding that in war everyone loses, but mostly those who never see those they love. This 'feminine' viewpoint further undergirds the fact that both masculine and feminine were part of the life of Israel and the spiritual relationship with God.

Huldah

Jerusalem, after years of being ruled by leaders who raised idols, offered pagan sacrifices and committed great sins, finally had a king who "did that which was right" (2 Chronicles 33:22). He began a cleanup campaign to bring the land back to the way it had been under his ancestor, King David. He broke down the idol altars, cleared the groves where the pagan rituals had taken place, and he sent his servants to take funds to the High Priest, Hilkiah, to repair the house of God.

During this repair, the High Priest found a "book of the law of the Lord given by Moses." After hearing its words, the king was greatly disturbed that the land had drifted from the words of the Lord. As a result, several ambassadors of the king went to Huldah, a prophet and the wife of the Shallum, keeper of the garments.

She lived in a region called the "Second Quarter", or what the KJV calls the "college." There were gates to the temple area named for this woman and the Midrash (Rabbinic commentaries on the Scriptures) clearly notes these were "*never destroyed*" and adds *"this was the gate where she sat and taught." [112]* Various sources suggest this part of the temple wall was the likely location of a prophetic school or office.

Some sources have attempted to marginalize or excise Huldah as a respected prophet and without evidence. They have suggested there was a library and Huldah 'merely' a chief librarian.[113] Other sources have denigrated her role as prophet/teacher/leader by suggesting she was the only one available and thus the envoy from the king had to settle for second best.[114] Still others suggest that Josiah sought merely to circumvent God's wrath, hoping a woman would temper the punishments. Over the decades, a combination of history, culture, and male dominated interpretation have effectively buried Huldah.

What the story says clearly is that, in the wake of the nationwide purging of pagan influences, she was one of

---

[112] *There is a comment added to Rashi's commentary on that verse in Melachim, suggesting that Chuldah taught... to the sages by that gate. (http://ohave.tripod.com/chumash/chuldah.htm).*

[113] "Huldah, Huldah, Prophetess or Librarian." At http://www.piney.com/Huldah.html. Accessed 11/5/2009.

[114] *NIV Study Bible.* Grand Rapids, MI: Zondervan, 1995, pg. 1734-1735

those in the city found to be still true to God. The pagan priests, temples, groves, and idols were gone but not Huldah or her established places near the gate. Biblical scholars are coming to understood that the prophets often had specific areas where they worked: some roamed, some were rural, and some lived in the city. Some, like Huldah, were part of the daily working of the temple and were no doubt involved in some type of formal training. At the Huldah gate may have been, as Jewish tradition suggests, a place where the prophetic and the scholarly met. People would have come to her, just as King Josiah ordered his ambassadors, so they might "...inquire of the Lord..." (2 Chron. 34:21).

Anna - Acts

In Luke 2:36-38 the prophet Anna serves to validate the authenticity of Jesus as promised Messiah.[115]   "... Anna, **a prophetess**, the daughter of Phanuel, of the tribe of Aser; she was of a great age..., but served God "[116] (KJV).   A

---

[115] Aune, David E. *Prophecy in early Christianity and the ancient Mediterranean world.* Grand Rapids, Michigan: Wm. B. Eermans, 1983, pg. 147.

[116] Holy Bible. King James Version

woman, in the opening days of the life of Jesus Christ, is shown to be serving in a spiritual role. She is clearly labeled a prophet, and is actively involved in proclamation. The significance of this simple scene cannot be over-stated. It argues clearly that during the period between the two testaments, women continued to be able to participate in the spiritual life of the community, were recognized as 'prophet', and were acknowledged by people who came to the temple.

In Acts 21:8-9 this tradition is continued --"...and we entered the house of Philip the evangelist ..... the same man had **four daughters,** virgins, **which did prophesy."**

In both of these examples, the term used refers to women who were inspired to foretell events, to act in the prophetic office, or be similarly inspired[117]. David Aune notes that the book of Acts lists more prophets than any other and it is significant that among those are these spiritually gifted women.[118]

The New Testament continues the tradition of the prophetic ministry of women from the birth of Christ to the birth of the church. It also suggests that commonly held

---

[117] Strong, James. *The New Strong's exhaustive Concordance of the Bible*. Nashville, Tennessee: Nelson, 1996, pg. 108.1.

[118] Aune, pg. 191.

understandings of the role of women in society and religious culture may be less rigidly defined than both Jewish and Christian commentaries often suggest. Moreover, it clear that all the women illustrated functioned, regardless of age or marital status, within these ministries areas termed "prophetic."

Corinth

The troubled church at Corinth communicated with the Apostle Paul around the year 55 C.E. Located on the isthmus connecting Greece to the mainland, the cosmopolitan city was a hive of busy commerce and a landscape of diverse cultures.119

1 Corinthians 11: 5 states that *"every woman that prayeth or prophesieth with her head uncovered dishonoureth her head."* People have been debating meanings and applications since the first century. What is clear, but often overlooked, is that Christian women were both praying in public and functioning in prophet like roles in the assembly. Paul's attempts to address issues of disorder, bad behaviors, and other problems that were making the church at Corinth poor

---

119 *NIV Study Bible*, pg. 1734-1735.

witnesses of Christ resulted in many faulty practices and illogical conclusions. [120]

Many who interpret this chapter see a limitation and muzzling of women in general. The letter, essentially a conversation of which only one side is known, responds to several previous communications. Covering numerous issues, Paul's' remarks are in the context of bringing solutions to specific local issues.

The revealing focus seen in the book all revolve around issues of control and authority. This divisive topic reveals the systemic issues of the troubled church at Corinth. As they discuss these scriptures or as Paul provides instruction the issues are clear.

Commentaries are frequently replete with words that emphasize woman being under "control", "rule", "hierarchy", "head", and "authority." Yet, these were words also reflecting the roots of the troubles in this ancient

---

[120] Hudson, Marilyn A. *Those Pesky Verses of Paul*. Norman, Oklahoma: Whorl Books, 2009. "Among the many questions raised in this section is to whom does Paul address his comments? Due to a lack of clarity in the Greek terms, it is unclear if Paul is speaking to only married people here or not. Contextually, however, it appears most likely he was addressing married couples. Despite this, some groups continue to interpret these words to mean that every woman, married or not, is under some man's "authority."

congregation. Why would Paul further seek to support the issues that were destroying the church at Corinth?

What is at fault is not the words, as some would suppose, but rather the continued misunderstanding of the words in balanced context with other Biblical texts. As Philip Noss has pointed, "...Bible translation is never innocent. There is always motivation for translation, and inevitably there are implications and consequences to the act of translation."[121] Habitual proof-texting supporting a hierarchy of authority, assigning value and power based on gender seems at odds with a gospel message that emphasized just the opposite. That is what is done in placing women in a secondary position without cause. As Fee and Keener point out, translating "head" to mean "leader" is an uncommon use of the Greek term.122

Some sources attempt to equate these actions of praying and prophesying as too similar to the cultic rituals of the Corinthian community. Others argue out that such actions violated some Roman, Corinthian, or Jewish rules of decorum. There is adequate evidence in Paul's' writings that

---

[121] Noss, Philip. *A History of Bible Translation*. Introduction.
[122] Keener, Craig. S. *Paul, Women, & Wives: Marriage and Women's Ministry in the Letters of Paul*. Peabody, MAS: Hendrickson's, 1992. pg. 32-33.

part of their problems stemmed from confusing actions or conflicting beliefs within the Christian community at Corinth. The issue of the type and nature of this supposed 'covering' is beyond the scope of this discussion.[123] Germaine to this discussion is that the actions of the woman (in praying or in prophesying) is not questioned, or condemned, but is accepted as the norm. It is an apparent accepted fact that women will be praying and 'prophesying' and indeed both Christ and Paul's wording supports this.[124]

The nature and function of this act of 'prophesy' is the focus here and although some do suggest that this "prophetic" speech was somehow less than authoritative, or of a different caliber, the argument appears forced and inconsistent with other examples in scripture.125 Conzelmann, and others, may be very correct in suggesting that here Paul is not making a pronouncement but merely

---

[123] Hudson, pg. 31, notes 71, 72, 73. Various translations (Mounce, Green, Berry) reflect their biases in 1 Cor.11.16 when they chose to translate 'toioutos' in reference to 'covering' by inserting "other" instead of "such." Thus, the verse 'we have no such custom" becomes "we have no other custom" with vastly different meaning.

[124]Strong, pg. 1081, Strong notes the term is the same in 1 Cor. 11.5, 1 Cor. 14.5 and the same as Jesus used in Mt.11.13 (#4395).

[125] Grudem, Wayne. *The Gift of Prophecy in 1 Corinthians*. Landham, MD: University Press, 1982.

citing remarks sent to him drawn from rabbinic sources, local comments, or Jewish custom.126 In essence, Paul is repeating their illogical, unscriptural, and fuzzy logic comments before he provides his answers. As noted earlier, there were numerous examples of prophetic women well into the time of the New Testament. Some even among the close families of Jesus' own disciples. Why would scripture now want to prohibit the practice?

Carthage

On a March morning in about the year 202, a twenty-two year old Christian woman walked onto the warm sands of the arena in Carthage, North Africa. There she and her companions were executed in a public spectacle. Her killer missed the first time. She cried out from the sword shoved between her ribs but, witnesses claimed, she then guided the 'wavering right hand of the youthful gladiator to her throat" to finish the task.[127]

---

[126] Conzelemann, Hans. *First Corinthians*. Philadelphia: Fortress, 1975, pg. 186-187; *The Interpreter's Bible*. Nashville; Abingdon, 1953, pg. 125-126.

[127] 'The Passion of the Holy Martyrs Perpetua and Felicitas." *The Anti-Nicene Fathers, translation of the writings of the Fathers down to A.D.*

Swept up in the purge of Septimus Severus and the edict outlawing conversion to Judaism or Christianity, it was this woman who had sustained the prisoners, who had stood up to her captors, and whose deep faith manifested through visions which sustained them as they awaited their martyrdom.[128] The source of this account is a unique and rare first person narrative of the events experienced by the woman until her death.[129] Such accounts in early church history are very rare yet this one is seldom noted in many works on the early church.[130] Devalued due to anti catholic biases, dismissed as a heretic, and otherwise ignored her presence has been minimized. The story stands out as a take of a brave woman of faith in the early church corpus.

---

325. Volume 3, Latin Christianity. Grand Rapids, Michigan: Wm. B. Eerdmans, 1976, pg. 699f.

[128] Jackson, Samuel Macauley., ed. *The Schaff-Herzog Encyclopedia of Religious Knowledge*. Volume VIII. Grand Rapids, MI: Baker Book House, 1959, pg. 466.

[129] McKechnie, Paul. The First Christian centuries: perspectives on the early church. Downer's Grove, Illinois: Intervarsity Press, 2001, p.172.

[130] Many of the sources consulted agreed she was significant but merely mentioned in passing or as an introduction to dissect her alleged relationship with Montanism. No definitive proof appears to support the charge and may be related to writings aimed at minimizing an alternate religious view and women's role in the fledging Roman Church.

Several things become apparent in examining *The Passion of Perpetua and Felicitas.*

First, Perpetua is recognized as having the gift of prophetic dreams. Dreaming was identified as a valid prophetic gift in the New Testament in the examples of Peter and then John on Patmos.[131] Her fellow captives asked her to use her gift "...that it may be made known to you whether this is to result in a passion or an escape."[132] She had apparently passed the Biblically accepted test of a true prophet in that her visions had come true.

It is clear from the writing and the esteem of the early church that she was not an anomaly but a role model for spirituality. She was a woman of strong faith, determination, and character to whom others looked for leadership. This is also seen in her responses to the repeated attempts of her pagan father to get her to recant and is clear in the way she alone appears to have confronted their jailor for better food and care.[133]

---

[131] Yocum, pg. 96. The author identifies other prophetic forms as being exhortation, visions, song, revelation, personal prophecy, actions, tongues and interpretation, private prayer (pg. 88-102).

[132] *Passion,* pg. 700.

[133] *Passion,* pg. 704.

Osiek and McDonald point out that in this time women were being mythologized into idealistic constructs, just as Judaism had done prior to the time of the New Testament in the Proverbs woman. As a result, 'real' women were being lost.[134] Perpetua, as a strong woman of faith, breaks with social mores of appropriate behavior. Instead of considering her spiritual strength, courage, and obvious gifting anomalous, however, they were repeated for centuries as models of piety for both genders.[135]

California

In 1907, a revival spread from a small mission on Azusa Street in Los Angeles, California. From humble beginnings, the activities and spiritual dynamic of that place would make its mark on the world. This event would become in essence a commissioning center launching what would become one of the twentieth century's most controversial movements, Pentecostalism. To this event, people came to observe and took back to their churches both reports and the experience of speaking in other tongues. With that went an acceptance of races, genders, the

---

[134] Osiekm Carolyn and Margaret Y. Macdonald. A *Woman's Place: House Churches in Earliest Christianity*. Fortress Press, 2006, pg. 229.
[135] Oden, Amy. *In Her Words: Women's writings in the History of Christian Thought*. Abingdon, 1994. Also, Blamires, Alcuin, et al. *Woman Defamed and Woman Defended: an anthology of Medieval texts*. Oxford, 1992.

experience of prophecy, the experience of signs and wonders not enjoyed in such an all encompassing a manner since the early church.

With strong roots in racial and sexual equality, the burgeoning Pentecostal movement grew as the result of its inclusion of both sexes as ministers and leaders. Cecil Robeck has astutely noted that Pentecostals justified their gender inclusion based on Joel 2:22 and that most other Protestants did so later only when forced by social pressures.[136]

In one of the services at the Azusa Street Mission, a Christian woman from Pasadena stood in a meeting, "I do not ask for tongues but I want to love God with all my heart and soul and my neighbor as myself," and she "immediately began to speak with tongues."[137] Her attitude was common of many who merely went to find more of Christ and in the process found a new spiritual dimension.

---

[136] Robeck, Cecil. The Azusa street mission and revival: the birth of the Global Pentecostal Movement. Nashville, Tennessee: Nelson, 2006, pg.15.

[137] Corum, Fred T., ed. *Like as of Fire, a reprint of the old Azusa Street papers*, Wilmington, Mass.: Fred Corum, 1981, pg. 20 (The Apostolic Faith .November 1906 : 2).

The emerging prophetic vision and leadership of women are well represented in this significant time of revival in the American church. Mrs. Mrytle K. Shideler, New York City, had an experience where she felt herself so under the thrall of the Holy Spirit that she was unable to move. Noting she did not faint or suffer from unconsciousness, she added, "He showed me things which there are not enough words in the English language to express. I do not wonder we need to cry, "O for a thousand tongues to sing my great Redeemer's praise.' The room and the people were hid from my senses and vision and JESUS walked in regal majesty, and His whole being was inexpressible and unutterable LOVE..."[138]

These early Pentecostals were often accused of being heretics, aligned with the devil, and dozens of other labels used to malign the participants. To be certain, there were occasional extremes before a common theology developed. This time of doctrinal void created many problems for the nascent revival movement. "Enthusiasms" was one of the kinder terms used to define these exuberant manifestations of spiritual contrition, joy and blessing. From shortly after the time of Perpetua, the early church and its 'enthusiasms' had been tamed, labeled primitive, and by the

---

[138] Corum, pg. 31 (The Apostolic Faith.(January 1907:3).

time of the birth of the 20th century, church was perceived as a place of culture, refinement and social order.

The impact of the Pentecostal outpouring was not merely in personal spiritual experiences but in the bestowal of various spiritual gifts and callings that were a challenge to the social order.[139] Racial, class, and gender equality were possible for participants in all aspects of the Pentecostal revival. Like Perpetua, many women experienced visions, became leaders, and bold messengers of faith. As is often the case people may plan but God moves as He sees fit. Florence Crawford in Oakland, California reported, "one night as I was weary in body, I asked the Lord to give me sleep, and he gave me a vision."[140]

Conclusion

What those early twentieth century Pentecostals experienced was similar to the experiences of ancient Israel, Christians in first century Corinth, and those striding into a second century arena. The stories of the realities of

---

[139] Cox, Harvey. *Fire from heaven.* Cambridge, Massachusetts: Da Capo Press, 1995, pg. 121.

[140] Corum, December 1906, pg. 4

prophetically gifted women in scriptures, and history, demonstrate the reality of spiritual leadership. From ancient times with Perpetua in Carthage, to reports of visions among the early Pentecostals, to the present, is revealed one long line of women functioning as full participatory members in the prophetic role. To this day, that heritage continues in the strong leadership and spiritual gifting of women in more recent Pentecostal and Charismatic settings.

Grant Wacker's *Heaven Below* notes that Pentecostalism continued to look to the Upper Room and to Joel 2:22 for both defense and mandate for their actions.[141] For all of these women, the issue was never politics, power, or equality. Eseldra Alexander states that the issues were awareness and acceptance so that, 'women fully qualified by the Spirit, could function without restraint alongside their male colleagues."[142]

From Old Testament to New Testament the precedent was in place revealing women serving God as chosen by their peers or led by the Spirit. From second

---

[141] Wacker, Grant. *Heaven below*. Cambridge, Massachusetts: Harvard, 2001, pg. 162-176.

[142] Alexander, Estrelda. *The Women of Azusa Street*. Cleveland, Ohio: The Pilgrim Press, 2005.

century revival movement to twentieth century, women continued to respond to the message of God in fervent faith, willing service, and sacrificial actions.

The continuum of women as prophets and servants of God is long, honorable and integrally meshed with the history of God's interaction with humanity and in particular in the liberating message of Pentecostalism.

PUBLISHING THE WORD – SHAPING THE MESSAGE:

A Survey of Publishing Influences in One Pentecostal Denomination, 1955 and 1965

Marilyn A. Hudson, M.L.I.S.

When Pentecostal Holiness Church minister, author, and publisher, George F. Taylor died in early 1935 his Bishop said of him, "he thirsted after knowledge…"[143] It is significant that in the midst of memorials praising his deep spiritual commitment and abiding faith that King would point out the obstacles the physically challenged man endured to make learning a reality.

It is noteworthy because of the anti-intellectualism charges often brought to bear against Pentecostals and other evangelical groups. [144] It may reflect the values both King and Taylor had concerning the life of the mind in spiritual life.[145] Early Pentecostals produced numerous schools, newspapers, and books suggesting they valued literacy to some extent but it also suggests a duality at work in the broader movement reflecting Hofstader's "cult of religious practicality." [146] The entire issue underscores the paucity of

---

[143] King, J.H. "He Being dead yet speaketh". Heb. 11:4. Pentecostal Holiness Advocate (Jan.10, 1935): 8. In the same issue, similar comments regarding the influence of his writing were made by Dan T. Muse and O.E. Sproull. A.H. Butler cited his dedication to the cause of a Christian based education.

[144] Hofstader, Richard. Anti-intellectualism in American life. New York: Vintage, 1963,pg. 264 refers to the American cult of practicality and pg. 67f discusses the negation of a learned ministry by some groups.

[145] Nanez, Rick M. Full Gospel, fractured minds? Grand Rapids, MI: Zondervan, 2005, pg. 85, 116f, 135f.

[146] Hofstader, Richard, pg.. 264.

information about the reading habits and influences among early Pentecostalism.

Augustine wrote that "a person who is a good and true Christian should realize that truth belongs to his Lord, wherever it is found..." [147] Despite being birthed in a Bible College at the dawn of the twentieth century, and fed by Bible and Training schools , early Pentecostalism would not agree.[148] Instead, a solid vein of fideism weaves itself through most early groups. This view would be in place until the schism of fundamentalist and evangelical groups in mid-twentieth century. Since attitudes define actions, it would continue to influence reading and book related activity during most of the twentieth century.

It is clear religious publishing played a significant role in the education, training, and indoctrination of ministers and lay leaders but many question remain unanswered. What works were deemed suitable for ministers to read? Do the books recommended to people serving as local leaders in Pentecostal churches say anything about the value of reading and learning? Are the theological and social influences consistent with stated theological stances? What

---

[147] Saint Augustine. On Christian Teaching II.75.
[148] Howard, Ethel E., The Winds of God, the story of the early Pentecostal days (1901-1914) in the life of Howard A. Goss. New York: Comet Press Books, 1958, pg. 26-27, 34-40.

theological or social influences do those choices reflect? In examining the church publications of the Pentecostal Holiness Church in the years 1955 and 1965, this work seeks to uncover initial answers for these questions allowing some preliminary conclusions about reading and theological influences.

The Pentecostal Holiness Church

The Pentecostal Holiness Church formed in 1911 through the merger of two earlier groups. Based primarily in the southeast, by the mid-century mark it was transitioning into a truly global denomination.[149]   Several early leaders, including J.H. King and George Taylor, were educated and friendly to the idea of education. [150]   A majority, however, were strongly influenced by an anti-learning bias derived from social forces of anti-modernism and negative personal experiences by many from "mainline churches" in the south opposed to the renewal movement. Both Synan and Nanez cite this prevailing attitude concerning education and

---

[149] Synan, The Old Time Power, 1998, pg. 316, 296,223.

[150] Bradshaw, Charles J. Profiles in Faith. Advocate Press, 1984, pg. 123f and 196f. See also Synan, Vinson, The Old-Time Power, Advocate 1998, pg. 58.

spiritual vitality being mutually exclusive. [151]   Attitudes have consequences by forging action or by approving inaction.

Although a leader of a group of people who were devout Christians and would himself echo the value of education, as early as 1928 then Bishop J.H. King bemoaned the fact so few preachers availed themselves of the Bible Conferences King was conducting. [152]

Joe E. Campbell in 1951 published the first history of the Pentecostal Holiness Church based on his dissertation, The Pentecostal Holiness Church 1898-1948: Its Background and History. [153]   It was a massive 573 pages divided into three parts. "Why the Pentecostal Holiness Church and Other Kindred Pentecostal and Holiness Groups Exist" presented an explanation and apologetic for such groups and dealt with the evolution of sects and denominations; the next section presented a formal history of PH divided into the denomination's early work to 1911

---

[151] Synan, The Old Time Power, 1998, pg. 38; Nanez,156,196f.

[152] King, J.H. "Comments" (Advocate, June 21, 1938, pg. 1) "...*as long as we have a ministry that does not study the word of God and have no interest in Bible Conference work, we will have stagnation and death where such may live and labor. A non-biblical ministry is loud, noisy, empty and inefficient. May there place soon be vacant.*"

[153] Campbell, Joe E. Pentecostal Holiness Church 1898-1948 : Its Background and History. Franklin Springs, GA: The Publishing House (PHC), 1951.

through the contemporary "Efforts and Expansion" developments. Finally, he examined the development of education and publishing within the PHC and noting they were important enough to warrant a "more comprehensive account."[154]

In his comments about the state of publishing in the PHC Campbell identifies issues common to most Pentecostal groups early in their development. Citing the existence of few published works, he ties this lack to issues of finances, lack of recognition of the value of such activity. He clearly ties writing into the matrix of spiritual gifts when he adds that those "capable of writing" have not "recognized their gift and made use of it." [155]He plainly stated another root cause for the lack of serious writing and reading among the people of the movement:

"The average person of the Pentecostal Holiness communion is not the type of person who has cultivated an appreciation for reading. On the whole they have not obeyed Paul's instruction to "give attendance to reading." (559).

With the dawn of the mid-century, the influences of evangelicalism were being felt across the country. Unlike some conservative religious groups, the Pentecostal Holiness

---

[154] Ibid, (xiv)
[155] Ibid, (559).

Church chose to join the National Evangelical Association and in doing so changed the course of their religious experiences and the summer in which the church would interact with society.[156] The NAE was formed in 1942 as a reaction to the influx of modernism, fundamentalism and the nascent council of churches. In aligning themselves with the NAE, the Pentecostal Holiness Church positioned itself to blaze a slightly different trail than some other groups.[157] The members of the NAE would go on to adopt middle of the road values of Christian worldview education, social action, and a willingness to open dialogue with diverse groups.[158]

The Publishers

Several theologically conservative publishers of the 1940-1960 periods became giants in filling a niche for evangelical and conservative works in the United States. The large reformed tradition churches were those who held to Calvinist doctrines. These included Presbyterians, Baptists, and others. In surveying the issues of the Pentecostal Holiness Advocate for the years specified identified specific

---

[156] Synan, The Old Time Power, pg. 222f
[157] Synan, Vinson. The Holiness-Pentecostal Movement in the United States. Eerdmans, 1971, p.207-8.
[158] Morrison, Robert L. "Ockenga, Harold" (pg. 607 and R.V Schnucker, "National Association of Evangelicals" (586). New 20th-century Encyclopedia of Religious Knowledge, 2nd ed. Grand Rapids: Baker, 1991.

publishers whose regularity of appearance gave them a high profile. They became part of a larger social process influencing literacy rates and education in the United States. Industry wide, in 1947 there were only 357 publishers in America and by 1973 that have grown to some 3,000 publisher. [159] Researchers have asserted the role of Christian publishing in aiding other positive social changes through its emphasis on publishing and mass education.[160]

Most publishers began in response to identified gaps in current publishing already in place. **William B. Eerdman** publishing began in 1911 with a target audience of Dutch farmers. They published many works, most by or about Calvin, by European scholars and first volumes were usually in the Dutch language. As they grew, they continued to reflect those reformed and conservative values as they switched to English language works.[161] **Baker Book House** and **Zondervan** emerged from similar backgrounds to Eerdman with similar reformed foundations and conservative views. **Moody,** an off shoot of the Moody

---

[159] Publishers Weekly Daily, at
http://www.publishersweekly.com/PWdaily/CA510344.html and
http://parapublishing.com/sites/para/resources/statistics.cfm
[160] Robert D. Woodberry and Timothy S. Shah. 2004. "Christianity and Democracy: The Pioneering Protestants." *Journal of Democracy.* 15(2): 47-61.

[161] "Eerdmans". A history, at
http://www.eerdmans.com/Pages/About.aspx; accessed 8/2/2012.

Bible Institute, originated in the late nineteenth century in response to a lack of Christian materials available to the public and to assist with their outreach efforts. Initially a rival, Baker in time even embraced the more general **Fleming J. Revell** as a subsidiary company. [162] **Advocate Press** (originally The Pentecostal Holiness Publishing House and now Life Springs Resources) launched in 1917 to meet the publishing needs of the six-year-old denomination.[163] Primarily it was concerned with a periodical for supplying news, testimonials, and announcements of denominational activity connecting the often-distant groups and ministers. As the needs of Sunday schools, revivals, and church departments grew, resources and news were shared on its pages related to missions, church planting, women's ministries, and continuing education. It published few books for the denomination beyond collections of sermons, study materials, or biographies of pioneers.

Questions of reading, book use, and education attitudes lead to issues of literacy in general. After the Civil War, 20 per cent of the American population fourteen and

---

[162] "Baker Book House Story", Baker, at
http://www.bakerbookretail.com/ME2/dirsect.asp?sid=7ED8499A12B7
44D7B7C3A9AE85E0F1E5&nm=History+of+Baker+Book+House ;
Revel Books, http://www.revellbooks.com/ME2; 'History of Moody
Bible Institute', Moody Publishers, at
http://www.moodyministries.net/crp_MainPage.aspx?id=62
[163] Bradshaw, pg. 198.

over could not read or write. Rates among African Americans and an unidentified "other" were excessively high in all years up to the mid century mark. Contrast to the rates at the birth of the modern Pentecostal movement in 1900 when the figure was 10.7 per cent and in 1910, three years after the Azusa Street revival in Los Angeles, the rate was 7.7 per cent of the total American population. In 1952, the year closest to the time surveyed in this study, it dropped to 2.5 per cent of the total American population. In 1969, the figure dropped to 2.2 per cent of the total. [164] Other studies, indicated correlations between reading skills and economic status and the period of this survey reflect an economic boom in American society.[165]

The realities of book purchasing and use also changed dramatically over the twentieth century adding to influences affecting reading. Today, anyone searching for a book has a vast range of easy avenues to find what they need. Options are numerous and include website catalogs,

---

[164] "120 Years of Illiteracy", National Assessment for Adult Literacy, National Center for Educational Statistics, at http://nces.ed.gov/naal/lit_history.asp#illiteracy based on U.S. Department of Commerce, Bureau of the Census, Historical Statistics of the United States, Colonial Times to 1970; and Current Population Reports, Series P-23, Ancestry and Language in the United States: November 1979.

[165] Adult Literacy in America, U.S. Department of Education, National Center for Education Statistics, National Adult Literacy Survey, 1992, pg. 61 accessed at http://nces.ed.gov/pubs93/93275.pdf

local mega bookstores, electronic downloads, academic and public libraries. During these decades surveyed, however, books were not as easy to locate. In 1954, for example, there were only 1,278 bookstores in America and in 1963, that number had grown only to 2,164. In comparison, by 2002 there over 10,000 bookstores dotted the United States.[166]

Additionally, bookstores of the era were often small and very general. Religious works were available in highly specialized stores designed to meet the needs of one religious view. *Baptist Book Stores* (Southern Baptist Convention) and Catholic Book shops emerged to supply the needs of their own diverse markets. It was not unusual for people during the 1950's and 1960's to travel to a nearby metropolitan or urban area in order to find a bookstore carrying religious works or to rely on mail orders for particular volumes.[167]

---

[166] Nord, David Paul, Joan Shelley Rubin and Michael Schudson. **The Enduring Book: Print Culture in Postwar America** , Book sales 1954 were listed as 771 million copies/ 7 million in sales. 1963 it as 1,035 million/ 2 million in sales. By 2002 sales were 26 million, page 509. Bookstores in 1954 , 1,278 and in 1963 2,164 in 2002 10, 860, page 514 ; later figures at U.S. Census, http://www.census.gov/econ/industry/hist/h451211.htm.

[167] Terry, Dennis R. Interview with the author, August31, 2011. Mr. Terry as a young minister in the early 1960's recalled the trips to the Christian bookstore in the nearest city were viewed as almost treats by most seeking to study and learn. "We saved our money to make a book buying trip or to order from a catalog."

Professional Reading in 1955

Scanning the pages of the 1955 and 1965 issues of the PHC Advocate it is clear the majority of book resources listed fell into distinct categories of material. These included professional resources, general church resources, and general interest.

Professional resources for the clergy were primary and included references for Biblical studies, sermon preparation, pastoral and doctrinal works. General church resources included materials for special ministries such as Sunday school, evangelism and children/youth. The smallest group included general interest titles such as fiction, poetry, or non-religious works. For the purposes of this study, the primary categories examined were materials in the area of professional resources and general interest.

Surveying the 1955 issue of the Pentecostal Holiness Church Advocate revealed approximately a dozen books recommended or advertised.[168] Their presence on the pages conveys the message the pastor or church leader should use such works as <u>Strong's Exhaustive Concordance</u>, Joseph

---

[168] The earliest issues contained ads or recommendations for books but usually only a few titles. A question remaining may be if the increases in titles profiled indicated a developing philosophy of improved literacy or merely an economic expediency of the publishing house.

Exell's <u>Biblical Illustrator</u> (Baker 1954), the <u>20th Century</u> <u>Encyclopedia of Religious Knowledge</u> (Baker), and the <u>Evangelical Sunday School Commentary (Higley, 1955)</u>. New and previous titles of the PHC were listed: Dr. Paul F. Beacham's <u>Questions and Answers</u> (PHC 1950) and Margaret Muse Oden's <u>Steps to the Sun (PHC, 1955)</u>, <u>An Orphan as Missionary</u> (PHC, 1952) and <u>The Pentecostal Message: sermons</u> (PHC, 1950). Of the resources listed, there was only one work of fiction, <u>Maid of Israel</u> by Tolbert R. Ingram (Broadman, 1955) and one song book, <u>Praise and Worship: A Gospel Hymnal</u> (Lillenas, 1950). The other titles included a work by the Kenyon movement's Samuel Dickson Gordon, <u>Treasury of Quiet Talks</u> (Baker, 1951) and Methodist Charles L. Allen's <u>When the Heart is Hungry</u> (Revell, 1955).

Helen Nelson penned an article directed more generally but which has bearing on the topic here, in "You Are What You Read" she reflected current prevailing concerns about juvenile delinquency. Although reflecting these concerns about the influence of certain types of reading, she still urged church members to actively participate in solving the problems thought to be produced through inferior reading choices. The influences of comic books and popular magazines would come providing "wholesome" and "age appropriate" reading materials through their churches and homes.[169]

Professional Reading in 1965

The decade of the sixties is one recognized as an explosive decade of cultural change. A time of colliding generations, fracturing social norms, and were, depending on viewpoint, either the devaluing of long held traditions or the formation of modern ones. Following a long decade of increasingly unsatisfying social conformity, as epitomized first in the 1955 Sloan Wilson work The Man in the Gray Flannel Suit and later in Betty Friedan's 1963 bestseller The Feminine Mystique, the sixties was definitely on a course of change. The tipping point came as youth reached their majority. It was a blast powerful enough to construct new mores through new ideas, challenges to the status quo, and a new moral value system. The church world was sometimes insulated and isolated but social reality. The size of this cultural shift was enough that eventually every religious group was challenged as changes from both within and without brought forces to bear on their concepts of faith in society.

---

[169] Nelson. Helen. "You are what you read." Advocate (Feb. 17, 1955): 5. A similar article appeared on pg. 8.

Surveying 1965, some of these changes are clear in the pages of the denominational publication. There were over fifty books prominently advertised, recommended, or otherwise presented as suitable for denominational membership to use. The works revealed several trends related to greater breadth of publishers used, balance of views, and variety within the presumed book buying audience.

Henry Ford's clever quip when marketing his new automobile, "you can have any color as long as it is black" would easily apply to the range of publishers used. [170] Readers could select any book as long as it was believed to be within the evangelical or conservative scope. Proportionally, the largest representation of publishers was still among those self-identified as reformed in theology and the largest group of authors whose theological stance was traceable can be identified as reformed. In addition, there was the prominent display of ads for the Scofield Reference Bible (1909). An interesting choice for a denomination self-defined in its theological stance as Wesleyan.

The lack of significant writings emerging from the denomination begs several questions as well. Given the fact

---

[170] Ford, Henry. My Life and Work. In collaboration with Samuel Crowther, 1922, New York, Classic Books, 2009, p. 72.

the denomination had passed its golden anniversary, only a few of the titles found in the 1965 issue were clearly identified as products of the writers or scholars of the Pentecostal Holiness Church. The few works clearly identifiable included <u>Songs of the Sanctuary</u>, Noel Brooks' <u>Sickness, Health & God</u>, Robinson's <u>Layman and the Book</u>, <u>Tips for Teaching</u>, Aaron's <u>Sermon Notes and Outlines</u>, and Morris' <u>Mark of the Beast</u>, H.P. Robinson's <u>Redemption Conceived and Revealed,</u> and Turner's <u>Rain over Hong Kong</u>.[171]   The publishers found to dominate the book selections were primarily works by Baker, Zondervan, Wm. B. Erdman's and Moody.

Theological Influences

For some authors, no biographical information or theological stance was located, but of those identified, they predominately represented Baptist, Presbyterian, Congregational and, to a lesser degree, Methodist positions. The placement of book advertisements or review columns with labels designating them as targeted for clergy, invite a presumption that they were the intended audience. Also presumed was that the primary audience of the "principal organ" of the denomination would continue to be the

---

[171] Jones, Charles E. <u>A Guide to the Study of the Pentecostal Movement</u>. Metuechen, NJ: Scarecrow Press, 1983. An invaluable set in identifying major works and authors in Pentecostal denominations.

church leaders (pastors, teachers, etc.) despite its inclusion of more general inspirational articles.

The relationship of reformed authors and publishers recommended in the PHC is initially unclear based solely on lists of books advertised. The mere presence of such works does not equate to influence in any measurable way. The goal of any inquiring or studious individual is to read well and to read widely. This is the core of being an educated person. The predominant presence of these authors and publishers, however, does suggest there may have been a growing theological duality emerging in the denomination.

While formally self-identifying as a Wesleyan-Arminian denomination with the first several articles of faith coming directly from the older Anglican Church, by way of the Methodist Church, there may have been on a popular level an emerging theological schizophrenia. Several forms and structures of polity had already shifted toward a congregational model of church government and away from the connectional ecclesiology model of early Methodism.[172]

---

[172] One example is the form of pastoral appointment , the call system rather than appointment by a bishop, reflecting its hybrid system of connectionalism which incorporates both local church self-governance and conferences; see Section IV. A. 1. "Organization in General", IPHC Manual 1993-1997, electronic edition.

What works were deemed suitable for ministers to read? Do the books recommended to people serving as local leaders in Pentecostal churches say anything about the value of reading and learning? With few exceptions, the works promoted appear to reflect what Hofstader termed the 'religious cult of practicality' that focused on applicability and practicality of learning and religion above any abstract elements.[173] The guiding premise being education, like art, could not be for its own sake but must reflect some more practical purpose or use. Nanez describes a similar attitude still among Pentecostals some forty years later as reflecting an "impoverishment" of modern culture.[174] Although the number of books, publishers, and literacy increased in the time from 1955 until 1965, Nanez points out lingering aversion among "full Gospel" people of taking on the heavy lifting of reading works that were more challenging or wrestling with critical thought. It becomes ironic that secular writers note an intellectual downsizing in American culture that comes close to reflecting the attitudes and results of the same thinking in Pentecostalism.[175]

---

[173] Hofstader, pg. 264-265.

[174] Nanez, 112-123.

[175] Jacoby, Susan. "The Dumbing of America," The Washington Post (17 Feb 2008) at http://www.washingtonpost.com/wp-dyn/content/article/2008/02/15/AR2008021502901.html ; Bauerlein, Mark. The Dumbest Generation. Tarcher , 2008;Keen, Andrew. The Cult of the Amateur. Doubleday, 2008.

Are the theological and social influences consistent with stated theological stances? What theological or social influences do those choices reflect?

Did the increasing presence of reformed tradition authors and publishers have an influence on the development of the theology and praxis of the PHC? Several factors might argue for this being the case.

The formation of the 'Women's Auxiliary' (1944), and its resultant minimizing of women in ministry and leadership, is sandwiched between denominational movements into the National Association of Evangelicals (1943) and then the Pentecostal Fellowship of North America (1948).

The general conferences of the 1940's through the 1950's saw both significant organizational infrastructure developed as well as near schisms due to doctrinal questions related to the emerging "full gospel", "salvation-healing" or "deliverance" ministries epitomized by people such as Oral Roberts and other people in the denomination.[176] While Roberts from an early point in his ministry utilized print and newer media to communicate, the standard for most ministers was still one of oral instruction through preaching

---

[176] Synan, Old Time Power, pg. 230-231.

or teaching. This adds a potentially inconsistent aspect to theological and organizational functionality.

The minimal presence of Methodist and Presbyterian authors and works (and the inferred Wesleyan-Arminian theological views) might be explained by fear of the growing liberal trends in those denominations. It is important to note, however, that even as new Methodist works declined, conservative Presbyterian works often remained. There does not appear to be a similar minimizing of clearly identified reformed tradition writers from Baptist perspectives and this may be due to a readiness among them to adopt the label of 'evangelical' despite possible negative connotations.

Although Synan would herald the role of the church periodical to mold the attitudes of the church during the era of the 1930's and 1950's, there was much left undone.[177] The reading level of the publication joined many other journals in lowering the reading levels of their periodicals. In the 1980's, the Advocate had an intentional reading level of 6th grade based on the 1948 Rudolph Flesch, author of Why Johnny Can't Read, developed a Magazine Chart.[178] Forerunner of the Flesch-Kincaid Readability Scale, this

---

[177] Synan, Old Time Power, pg. 204.

[178] Flesch R (1948). "A new readability yardstick". Journal of Applied Psychology 32: 221–233; author interview with the then editor, Shirley Spence, 1986, who cited standards of the Evangelical Press Association.

chart would rate the periodical at the same level as the 1940's "slick fiction" and just above comic books. A more recent scale likens the level to consumer ads. [179] While experts have differed over the accuracy or usefulness of the scales, they continue in use and provide valuable insight into reading in a society. [180] Campbell's early descriptions of the reading nature of the denomination were apparently still applicable thirty years later.

The dominant voice in the reference and reading of Pentecostal Holiness Church clergy and leaders, as seen in the pages of the official publication between 1955 and 1965, were authors or publishers specializing in reformed theologies rooted more in the work of John Calvin than the works of John Wesley. The common "voice" was becoming as much evangelical as distinctly Pentecostal.

As with many research projects the results often lead to more questions. Such is the case in the issue of influences and attitudes of reading in the Pentecostal Holiness Church. To identify and trace the development of any hybrid

---

[179] Flesch-Kincaid Readibility Scale, http://www.essociatesgroup.com/enformation_central/tools/Flesch%20 %20%20Test.pdf

[180] McClure G (1987). "Readability formulas: Useful or useless. (an interview with J. Peter Kincaid.)". IEEE Transactions on Professional Communications 30: 12–15; Farr JN, Jenkins JJ, Paterson DG (October 1951). "Simplification of Flesch Reading Ease Formula". Journal of Applied Psychology 35 (5): 333–337.

Wesleyan-Calvinist doctrine in the denomination or its polity, require more research. Such an exploration would also serve to clarify influences in issues of reading and learning among both clergy and laity.

The *Advocate* helped to publish the word and by their choices in books highlighted helped shape the message of the denomination. Just what the message was and how it may have helped to create new generations of people, who were like Taylor were 'thirsty for knowledge', is a subject worthy of further and wider study.

Appendix   Chart of Titles Surveyed

1955, PHC Advocate

Author	Title	Publisher/Date	Theology
	Evangelical SS Commentary	Higly, 1955	Evangelical
	Praise & Worship: Gospel Hymnal	Lillenas, 1950	
Egermeir	Egermeir's Bible Story Book	Warren, 1939	Holiness/Church of God
Beacham, P.F.	Meat in due season	PHC, 1954	Pentecostal
Oden, M.M.	Steps to the Sun	PHC, 1054	Pentecostal
Strong, et al	Strong's Exhaustive Concordance	1890	Methodist
Beacham, P.F.	Questions and Answers	PHC, 1954	Pentecostal
Gordon, S.D.	Treasury of Quiet Talks	Baker, 1951	Kenyon Movement
Allen, Charles L.	When the Heart is Hungry	Revell, 1955	Methodist
Ingraham, Tolbert R.	Maid of Israel	Broadman, 1955	Baptist
Exell, Joseph S.	Biblical Illustrator	Baker, 1954	Methodist

1965, PHC Advocate

Author	Title	Publisher/Date	Theology
	Wesleyan Bible Commentary	Eerdmans, c1950	Methodist/Holiness
Clark, Adam	Clark's Commentary	Various reprints, 1831	Methodist
	Revell's Ministry Manual	Revell, 1960	Reformed
	Hitchcock Topical Bible /Cruden's	Baker, 1956	Congregational
	Evangelical SS Commentary	Higby, 1965	Evangelical
Spurgeon	Morning and Evening Devotions	Zondervan, 1955	Baptist
Johnstone, Patrick G.	Rainbows and resurrection.		Presbyterian
	Songs of the Sanctuary	PHC	Pentecostal
Girod, Gordon H.	Words and Wonders of the Cross	Baker, 1962	Reformed
Holt, John A.	Seven Words	Zondervan, 1961	
Blackwood, Andrew J.	The Voice from the Cross	Baker, 1955	
Hobbs, Herschel H.	Crucial words from Calvary	Baker, 1958	Baptist
Jones,	Gold from Golgotha	Moody, 1945	

Russell B.			
Turnbull, Ralph G.	Seven words from the cross	Baker, 1954	Presbyterian
Pink, Arthur W.	Seven sayings of Jesus on the Cross	Baker, 1954	
Grant, J. Ralph	The Way of the Cross	Baker, 1963	
Doerffler, Alfred	Cross still stands	Baker, 1960	
Todd, G. Hall	Culture and the cross	Baker, 1957	
Deal, Wm S.	The soul Winner's Guide	Zondervan, 1961	
Hargrove, H.H.	Personalities around the cross	Baker, 1963	
Meyer, F.B.	Calvary to Pentecost	Baker, 1959	Baptist
Demaray, Donald E.	Loyalty to Christ	Baker, 1958	Free Methodist
MacLaren, Alex et al	Great sermons on the resurrection	Baker, 1963	Baptist
Todd, G. Hall	O Angel of the Garden	Baker, 1961	
Hobbs, Hershel H.	Messages on the resurrection	Baker, 1959	
Gager, Leroy	Handbook for soul winners	Zondervan	
Alexander, J.A.	Commentary on the Book of Acts	Zondervan, 1956 (1875)	
Godet, F.L.	Commentary on the	Zondervan 1955	Swiss Free

	Gospel of John		Evangelical
Murray, Alfred L.	Psychology for Christian teachers	Round Table, 1938	
Lee, Robert G,	Choice Pickings	Zondervan, 1961	
Lee, M.W.	So You Want to Speak	Zondervan, 1961	
Foushee, C.G.	Object lessons for Youth	Zondervan, 1945	Baptist
Emerson. Laura S.	Effective readings for special occasions	Zondervan, 1961	
	Scoffield Reference Bible		Presbyterian
Aaron, T.L.	Sermon Notes and Outlines	PHC	Pentecostal
Moore, H.L.	Mark of the Beast		
Bromiley and Henry	Baker's dictionary of theology	Baker,	
Cox, George	John Wesley's concept of Perfection.	Beacon Hill,	
Robinson, A.E.	Layman and the Book	PHC,	
Feinberg, Charles L.	Focus on prophecy,	Revell	
Leavitt, Guy	How to be a better Church Officer		

Howell, B.C.	Come alive!		
Pfeiffer, Charles F.	New Combined Bible dictionary and concordance		Baptist
Whiston, Wm	The Works of Josephus		
Tenney, Merrill	Zondervan Pictorial Bible Dict	Zondervan	Baptist
Douglas, J.D.	New Bible Commentary		
Davidson, F.	New Bible Commentary		
Young, Robert	Young's analytical concordance		Free Church. Presbyterian
Schafer, Wilma	Devotions and dialogues for women		
Elliot, Elizabeth	My Savage kinsman		Baptist
Morgan, G. Campbell	The Child and the Bible		Baptist
Brooks, Noel	Sickness, Health, and Healing	PHC/Advocate	Pentecostal
Robinson, H.P.	Redemption conceived and revealed		Pentecostal
	Tips for teaching	PHC/Advocate	Pentecostal
Cook, Howard R.	Intro to the study of missions		
Turner,	Rain over Hong Kong	PHC/Advocate	Pentecostal

Mosaic :

W.Holmes			
Whitsell, F.D.	Great Expository Sermons		
Nash, Ronald H.	New evangelicalism	Zondervan	Baptist
Jacobs, Vernon	81 Short speeches for 44 occasions		
Havner, Vance	Why Not just be Christians?	Revell	Baptist
Van Ness, Bethann	The Bible Story Book,		
Henry, Matthew	Matthew Henry's Commentaries		Presbyterian

WORKS CONSULTED

Anderson, Robert M. Vision of the disinherited: the making of American Pentecostalism. Peabody, Massachusetts: Hendrickson, 1979.

Bradshaw, Charles E., ed. Profiles in faith. Advocate Press, 1984.

Brown, Candy Gunther. The Word in the World: Evangelical writing, Publishing and Reading in America, 1789-1880.

Hofstader, Richard. Anti-intellectualism in American life. New York: Vintage Books, 1963.

Marsden, George M. Fundamentalism and American Culture.

Nanez, Rick M. Full gospel, fractured minds? Zondervan, 2005.

Nord, David Paul Nord, Joan Shelley Rubin, Michael Schudson. **The Enduring Book: Print Culture in Postwar America**

Thinking in Tongues: Pentecostal Contributions to Christian Philosophy (Pentecostal Manifestos) by James K. A. Smith (Jun 15, 2010)

Sweeny, Douglas A. The American Evangelical Story: a history of the movement.

Synan, Vinson. The Holiness-Pentecostal Tradition: Charismatic Movements in the Twentieth Century. 1997.

Synan, Vinson. The Old Time Power. LifeSprings, 1998.

Wacker, Grant. Heaven Below: Early Pentecostals and Culture.

ABOUT THE AUTHORS

DR. CHRIS GREEN

Dr Chris Green, is currently serving as Assistant Professor of Theology at Pentecostal Theological Seminary in Cleveland, TN. Previously, he taught at Oral Roberts University in Tulsa, and Southwestern Christian University in Bethany, OK, while holding adjunct positions at other schools in the Oklahoma City area. Dr Green and his wife, Julie, helped plant and pastor a church in Northwest Oklahoma City, in 2003. After stepping down from that role, they moved to Cleveland, TN to teach at the Seminary. Dr. Green completed his PhD in theology (Bangor University, Wales) and previously received a Doctorate of Ministry (D.Min.) from ORU. He also has a Master's degree in theology, and Church Leadership. They have two kids: Zoe, 7, and Clive, 4. He is author of <u>Toward a Pentecostal Theology of the Lord's Supper: Foretasting the Kingdom</u> (2012).

REV. KENNETH L. YOUNG

Ken L. Young is a Professor of Bible and Theology at Southwestern Christian University in Bethany, Oklahoma. He served also for fourteen years as the Dean of Adult Studies. Ken represents a fourth generation Pentecostal Holiness heritage. His father, maternal grandfather and great grandfather were ministers in the Pentecostal Holiness movement. Ken holds ministerial credentials through the Upper South Carolina Conference of the International Pentecostal Holiness Church. Ken pastored two churches in South Carolina for a total of eight years while serving on the Conference World Missions Board and the Conference Evangelism Board. He is currently a candidate for the Doctor of Ministry.

IRENE BELYEU, AUTHOR

In 1929, Irene Barbara Parris was born into a loving family near Shawnee, Oklahoma. Irene spent her childhood working in the fields and woods and walking to school and to church. She reveled in the beauty of nature in the earth and the sky. In 1950, she was married to Darrell Belyeu and had six children. Irene began an intensive study of the Book of Revelation to answer her children's questions as well as her own. At the age of fifty-six, she completed a Bachelor of Arts degree in linguistics from the University of Oklahoma and was elected to Phi Beta Kappa. A volunteer tour with the Wycliffe Bible Translators gave her insight into translation and literacy. She applied her linguistic training to research on the Book of Revelation and, as a result, has published, <u>Revelation in Context</u> (2012). Her sermons are available at <u>www.sermon.net/revelationincontext</u>.

DR. MARVIN J.HUDSON

Dr. Marvin J. Hudson, ordained minister, holds the D.Min. from Asbury Theological Seminary and the Master of Arts from Southern Nazarene University and a Master of Divinity from Phillips Theological Seminary. He is certified as an Intentional Interim Ministry Specialist. He has taught Biblical languages, Theology, Biblical studies, and Leadership in several institutions. He is a member of the Society of Biblical Literature and the South Central Classics Association.

MARILYN A. HUDSON, AUTHOR

Marilyn A. Hudson is a professional in the fields of history, library and information having received degrees from the University of Oklahoma. Additionally she is an author, educator, professional storyteller, workshop leader and speaker. Her published works include *Those Pesky Verses of Paul* (2011) and *Noel Brooks: a Life Shining and Burning* (2011). She is a member of the Association of College and Research Libraries, the South Central Classics Association, and the Oklahoma Library Association.

www.ingramcontent.com/pod-product-compliance
Lightning Source LLC
Chambersburg PA
CBHW072005040426
42447CB00009B/1489